Better Homes and Gardens®

Christmas
Comfort & Joy

501 crafts, decorating,
and food ideas to
make your holiday
unforgettable

Better Homes and Gardens® Books
Des Moines, Iowa

Better Homes and Gardens® Books
An imprint of Meredith® Books

Christmas — Comfort & Joy

Editor: Carol Field Dahlstrom
Contributing Writer: Susan M. Banker
Graphic Designer: Angela Haupert Hoogensen
Copy Chief: Terri Fredrickson
Copy and Production Editor: Victoria Forlini
Editorial Operations Manager: Karen Schirm
Managers, Book Production: Pam Kvitne, Marjorie J. Schenkelberg
Contributing Copy Editor: Margaret Smith
Contributing Proofreaders: Carol Boker, Sheila Mauck, Sherri Schultz
Technical Illustrator: Chris Neubauer Graphics, Inc.
Electronic Production Coordinator: Paula Forest
Editorial and Design Assistants: Kaye Chabot, Mary Lee Gavin, Karen McFadden

Meredith® Books
Editor in Chief: James D. Blume
Design Director: Matt Strelecki
Managing Editor: Gregory H. Kayko

Director, Sales, Special Markets:
Rita McMullen
Director, Sales, Premiums:
Michael A. Peterson
Director, Sales, Retail: Tom Wierzbicki
Director, Book Marketing: Brad Elmitt
Director, Operations: George A. Susral
Director, Production: Douglas M. Johnston

Vice President and General Manager:
Douglas J. Guendel

Better Homes and Gardens® Magazine
Editor in Chief: Karol DeWulf Nickell

Meredith Publishing Group
President, Publishing Group:
Stephen M. Lacy
Vice President–Publishing Director: Bob Mate

Meredith Corporation
Chairman and Chief Executive Officer:
William T. Kerr

Chairman of the Executive Committee:
E. T. Meredith III

All of us at Better Homes and Gardens® Books are dedicated to providing you with information
and ideas to create beautiful and useful projects. We welcome your comments and suggestions.
Write to us at: Better Homes and Gardens Books, Crafts Editorial Department,
1716 Locust Street—LN112, Des Moines, IA 50309-3023.

If you would like to purchase any of our crafts, cooking, gardening, home improvement,
or home decorating and design books, check wherever quality books are sold. Or visit us at: bhgbooks.com

Cover Photograph: Andy Lyons Cameraworks

Our seal assures you that every recipe in *Christmas — Comfort & Joy* has been tested in
the Better Homes and Gardens® Test Kitchen. This means that each recipe is practical
and reliable, and meets our high standards of taste appeal. We guarantee your satisfaction
with this book for as long as you own it.

"The joy of brightening other lives, bearing each other's burdens, easing others' loads and supplanting empty hearts and lives with generous gifts becomes for us the magic of Christmas." —W.C. Jones

Lights are twinkling around us, snowflakes are in the air, and children are keeping secrets and giggling with anticipation. Christmas is upon us and we rejoice in this most beloved of all holidays.

What better time to bring comfort and joy to the ones you love than during the Christmas season. In this big book of festive ideas we share ways to decorate your home, ideas for making gifts for the ones you love, and recipes to make goodies from your kitchen. From holly wreaths and jeweled centerpieces to clever ornaments and knitted sweaters, these ideas and projects will turn your home into a holiday retreat. Your kitchen will be a favorite place to gather as you create holiday breads, hearty soups, and oh-so-sweet candies and cookies. Your Christmas tree will sparkle with handmade trims as it reflects your festively decorated home. Your gifts will be remembered more because you made them yourself and we'll give you ideas for everyone on your Christmas list.

So celebrate this holiday knowing you are bringing the very best to your family and friends—your love and talent for their comfort and joy.

Carol Field Dahlstrom

Contents

Let Heaven & Nature Sing

"The merry family gathering—the old, the very young; the strangely lovely way they harmonize in carols sung. For Christmas is tradition time—traditions that recall, the precious memories down the years, the sameness of them all."

—Helen Lowrie Marshall

Happy Holly Trims

Holly Wreath

WHAT YOU NEED

Yardstick; newspapers; black marking pen
Heavy wire or sticks, optional
Wire cutter; floral wire; fresh holly
4 red plastic cookie cutters

HERE'S HOW

1 To make a wreath to frame a window, measure the window and add 4 inches to each measurement. Draw this shape on newspapers to follow as a guide.

2 For large wreaths, cut heavy wire or sticks the size of the drawn guide to use as a foundation. Arrange holly pieces on ruled guide, overlapping the stems, to achieve the desired look. Use a wire cutter to cut 8-inch lengths of wire. Wrap the wire around the overlapped stems to secure. If using a wire or stick foundation, wire the holly to the foundation as you work. Use wire to attach a cookie cutter to each corner. Trim excess wire. Add wire hangers to the top two corners.

Cookie Cutter Trim

WHAT YOU NEED

Red plastic cookie cutter; drill and $\frac{1}{16}$-inch bit
10-inch length of red small-gauge wire
Assorted glass beads; holly

HERE'S HOW

1 Drill a hole on each side of the cookie cutter. Thread the wire through one of the holes and secure.

2 Thread the beads onto wire, leaving about 2 inches of the wire remaining. Thread the remaining end of wire through the opposite hole. Twist to secure the wire.

3 Hang the trim on the doorknob and embellish it with holly behind the beaded wire.

Holly and cookie cutters make these inviting holiday displays. Look around your house to find a spot that needs a little holiday cheer.

Fruity Pursuit

Create a focal point on your buffet table with a medley of fruits piled high on a crystal plate. Pears, plums, kumquats, blueberries, and cranberries provide a regal mix of colors and textures. The graceful arrangement features fresh fruit, but artificial fruit may be easily substituted.

WHAT YOU NEED

Table knife
12-inch-tall green plastic-foam cone with 4-inch base
Toothpicks
Wood glue
Miniature artificial or fresh pears and plums, kumquats, blueberries, and cranberries
Grape leaves
Footed crystal cake plate or compote

HERE'S HOW

1 Use a table knife to trim off the tip of a plastic-foam cone. Put a generous amount of wood glue on the entire length of a toothpick. Insert one end of toothpick into a pear and the opposite end into top of cone. Continue attaching pears to cone in rows, working from top to bottom.

2 Fill in gaps between pears with miniature plums, then kumquats, attaching them in the same manner as the pears.

3 Finish with blueberries and cranberries, using toothpicks cut in half to attach.

4 Randomly tuck grape leaves into arrangement, dabbing glue on stems to secure in place.

5 When cone is covered with fruit as desired, let glue dry. Place the cone on a crystal compote.

Lime Lights

WHAT YOU NEED

1 to 2 cases of kumquats
1 to 2 dozen each of lemons, limes, and other desired
  citrus fruits
Dental floss; darning needle
Fine-gauge floral wire; wire cutter
Sheet moss; hyacinth sticks
Lemon leaves

HERE'S HOW

1 Create several garlands by stringing kumquats on a needle threaded with a single strand of dental floss. Leave extra floss on both ends.

2 Tie the ends of floss to chandelier, linking swags from light to light. Secure floss around the light base.

3 Decorate the connecting joints with lime halves. Cut limes in half; run floral wires through the backs and attach to joints with the wire. Wet small amount of sheet moss, squeeze out water, and tuck in around lime half. As the moss dries, it will expand and hide the joints.

4 Decorate the lights or candles with lemon leaves. Shape the leaves to the light base; string wire around the base to secure. Hide the wire with a small string of kumquats.

5 To make the leaf-and-fruit base, wire together lemon leaves to form small clumps; wire clumps together to form short garland. Loop the garland inside the chandelier base, forming a cradle for fruit. Secure fruit with wire.

6 Skewer some of the smaller fruit with hyacinth sticks and then wedge into the leaf-and-fruit base. Cut some lemons and limes in half for visual interest. Poke hyacinth sticks in kumquats and then wedge into the larger fruit arrangement. Cover the upper area of the chandelier with lemon leaves.

This chandelier, strung with kumquat garlands and accented with lemon leaves and fresh citrus, is a bold centerpiece for holiday meals.

Fireplace Magic

WHAT YOU NEED

**Wire wreath form; small magnolia branches
Medium-gauge floral wire; hyacinth sticks, optional
45 assorted pears for wreath or 60 for garland
Small nails; hammer; wire cutter**

HERE'S HOW TO MAKE THE WREATH

1 To make leaf base for wreath, cluster magnolia branches into groups of three, wiring together at stem. Wire clusters to wreath form, fitting each cluster tightly into the previous cluster; work in at a slight angle. Fill in wreath with leaf clusters.

2 Add fruit, using floral wire or hyacinth sticks. To attach with wire, work wire through center of fruit, leaving extra wire to secure to frame. Place fruit on wreath at angles; attach with the wire. To attach with hyacinth sticks, skewer fruit with the sticks; wedge the sticks into the frame.

HERE'S HOW TO MAKE THE GARLAND

1 Cluster magnolia branches into groups of three, wiring together at stems. Working at a slight angle, fit each cluster tightly into the previous cluster; wire. Form garland to the desired length.

2 Place small nails diagonally in the corner where mantel meets wall. Drape the garland over the mantel; hold in place with the nails. Shape garland.

3 Attach fruit with wire or hyacinth sticks in clusters, with several fruits attached randomly between.

4 To attach with wire, work wire through center of fruit, leaving extra wire to secure to garland. Place fruit on garland at different angles; attach with wire. To attach with hyacinth sticks, skewer fruit with the sticks; wedge into the garland.

Nontraditional holiday colors —green and orange— inspired this rich hearth setting. Far from monotonous, the magnolia-leaf wreath and garland are accented with a bushel full of fruit.

Fresh from the Woods

Give your kitchen a lift this holiday season with fresh flowers and greenery. Assemble wintry arrangements using aluminum buckets and clear vases filled with an array of white blooms, cranberries, and fresh greenery.

WHAT YOU NEED

Cranberries
Wide-mouth glass bowl
White large-head flowers,
    such as calla lilies, delphiniums, roses, and tulips
Geranium leaves
Crab apples
Hyacinth sticks
Gold wire-edge organza ribbon, if desired
Floral wire

HERE'S HOW

1 Fill a wide-mouth bowl with cranberries and water.

2 Using the cranberries as a base, add flowers and geranium leaves in clumps. Keep flower height low and close to rim.

3 If desired, add fruit to arrangement by skewering crab apples or other small fruits with hyacinth sticks; place fruit in clusters around arrangement.

4 If desired, finish with a bow. To make the bow, use a long length of wire-edge ribbon. Cut ends diagonally. Fold ribbon in half. About 2 inches from fold, hold ribbon between fingers, creating a loop. Make two additional loops on each side of center loop, making each slightly larger. Bunch bottom of loops and wrap tightly with wire. Release and arrange ribbon loops. Attach to bowl with wire.

Seasonal Stair Runner

A runner of greens is a step above the standard stair embellishment. This garland — made from evergreen branches and accented with individual pots of blooming white narcissus — lines the stairway.

WHAT YOU NEED

Cedar and mixed greens, or a purchased evergreen garland
Medium-gauge floral wire; wire cutter
White narcissus in small pots
Pinecones
White tulips, if desired
Large-leaf ivy
Gold wire-edge ribbon

HERE'S HOW

1   Construct the garland for stairs from cedar and mixed greens. Wire a handful of greens together. Arrange greenery clumps at right angles to each other; wire together for the length and fullness desired.

2   Lay garland along wall. Place potted narcissus amid garland; conceal pots with pinecones and extra greenery.

3   Prepare additional lengths of garland for the railing. Wire the garland lengths to drape vertically. Top with clumps of tulips and large, glossy ivy leaves secured with wire.

4   Embellish with wire-edge ribbon bows. To make the bows, cut ends diagonally. Fold ribbon in half. About 3 inches from fold, hold ribbon between fingers, creating a loop. Make two additional loops on each side of center loop, making each slightly larger. Bunch bottom of loops; wrap tightly with wire. Release the ribbon loops; position the loops as desired. Attach with wire.

Rose Wreath

WHAT YOU NEED

18-inch wet-foam wreath
Chicken wire
Florist's scissors
Wire cutter
250 to 300 red roses (look for different sizes, varieties, and hues)
2 bags of moss or 2 bunches lemon leaves, if desired

Fresh red roses packed tightly in a wreath create a colorful welcome.

HERE'S HOW

1 Cut chicken wire into a long, narrow strip; wrap around wet-foam wreath, twisting long edges around each other to secure. Soak wreath in water until saturated. Cut rose stems 3 to 4 inches long. Stick roses in foam wreath, placing the flowers close together to hold them in place. Experiment with the size, hue, and variety of the roses to create the desired effect.

2 To finish the back of the wreath (if you plan to hang it on a glass door, for example), cover the surface with moss or lemon leaves. To finish with moss, wet small moss bundles, squeeze out water, and wedge into the chicken wire. Cover the entire surface with the moss, which will expand as it dries. To finish with lemon leaves, bunch several leaves together; wire. Wire leaf bunches to the wreath base, covering the entire surface.

3 Maintain the wreath by removing faded or wilted flower heads and replacing them with fresh ones. Do not mist the wreath, which may cause molding. If conditions permit, allow roses to dry to be reused. The wreath should last 10 days to two weeks in temperate outdoor weather.

Natural Beauties

Watering Can Centerpiece

WHAT YOU NEED

Antique watering can
White tulips
Fir branches
Seeded eucalyptus

HERE'S HOW

1 For a simply elegant and fragrant centerpiece, fill an
antique watering can halfway with water. Add white
tulips, fir branches, and seeded eucalyptus.

*Deck your halls
with these lovely
arrangements,
which are ripe
for the making
with produce,
plants, and
materials from
local florists.*

Heather Tree

WHAT YOU NEED

Floral foam
Small galvanized bucket
Table knife
Branches of heather
**Sprigs of variegated
    mini pittosporum**
Ribbon
Scissors

HERE'S HOW

1 Place a block of wet floral
foam in the base of a
galvanized bucket. Using a
table knife, trim the foam to
¼ to ½ inch above the rim.
Secure branches of heather
and sprigs of pittosporum in
the foam. Wrap a coordinating ribbon around
the bucket and tie a bow.

Orange Topiary

A colonial-era classic, the fruit topiary is given a fresh twist with blood oranges and a metal French flowerpot.

WHAT YOU NEED

Block of floral foam; pot
Three ¼-inch wood dowels
Plastic-foam cone, such as Styrofoam
Sheet moss
Sharp knife; blood oranges or navel oranges
18-gauge copper wire
Ribbon

HERE'S HOW

1 Place a block of floral foam in the pot. Insert three ¼-inch wooden dowels in the bottom of a plastic-foam cone. Place the cone on the pot, inserting the dowels into the floral foam.

2 Cover the cone with damp sheet moss. Slice blood oranges in half (if unavailable, use navel oranges). Starting at the bottom of the cone, secure each orange half to the plastic foam with V-hooks made from 18-gauge copper wire as shown, *below.*

3 Fill in exposed areas with moss. Tie a glimmering ribbon into a bow to trim the topiary, allowing the ends to cascade.

Natural Combination

Use fresh fruits to string a colorful garland to decorate mantels, trees, staircases, or to wind through unusual potted candles.

WHAT YOU NEED

Kumquats
Blueberries or cranberries
Thin copper or florist's wire
Wire cutter
Darning needle
Candles
Whitewashed flowerpots
Grass-like plants or seeded grass in pots

HERE'S HOW

1 For garland, thread fresh fruits onto thin copper wire or florist's wire, using a large needle. Snip the wire at the desired length and twist a knot to secure fruit on each end of the fruit chain.

2 Nest candles in the flowerpots, arranged three or more in a row. Wind the garland among the pots of grass-like plants or seeded grass.

NOTE: *At room temperature, the chain will stay fresh two to five days.*

Raspberry Accents

Colorful Wreath

WHAT YOU NEED

Florist's wire
Sprigs of heather
Grapevine wreath
Ribbon
Scissors

HERE'S HOW

1 Wire sprigs of heather to a grapevine wreath. Add a touch of softness with a coordinating bow.

Berry Lights

WHAT YOU NEED

Hot-glue gun; hot-glue sticks
Small plastic candleholder to fit in small flowerpot
Small and large glass flowerpot
Taper candle
Moss
Fresh raspberries

HERE'S HOW

1 Hot-glue a plastic candleholder inside the bottom of a small glass flowerpot. Insert a candle in the holder. Fill in between the candle and the side of the flowerpot with moss. Arrange fresh raspberries around the top of the pot. Place the small glass pot into a larger glass flowerpot. Fill in the space between the pots with moss.

Raspberry hues add freshness to holiday decor. A heather wreath, opposite, brightens a window with cheery color. Berry candleholders create a festive look for a table or windowsill.

Pinecone Tiebacks

Bring woodland beauty indoors by fashioning these curtain tiebacks from nature's offerings.

WHAT YOU NEED

2 large pinecones
Gloss protective coating spray
Ice pick
2 screw eyes
24 inches of narrow gold wire-edge ribbon
1½ yards of gold cord
Hot-glue gun; hot-glue sticks
**Small pinecones, dried pods, leaves, or other natural
   small items to embellish large pinecones**

HERE'S HOW

1 Spray the pinecones with gloss coating and allow to dry.

2 Use an ice pick to poke a hole in the top of each large
   pinecone. Insert a screw eye into the hole and twist into
   the pinecone to secure.

3 Slip a 12-inch piece of ribbon through the screw eye.
   Tie a knot at one end of the cord. Before tightening the
   knot, slip one end of the ribbon through the knot and tie
   the ribbon tightly around the knot, pulling the knot next
   to the screw eye. Repeat to attach the second pinecone
   to the opposite end of the cord.

4 Hot-glue the knots to the tops of the pinecones. Glue
   additional pinecones, leaves, pods, or other natural items
   to the top of the pinecones.

Earthly Elegant Topiary

Even if you're frazzled from the holiday hoopla, you'll have time to craft this simple topiary that takes its cue from Mother Nature. Silvery accents sparkle from a moss-covered cone supported by a tree branch. This tabletop Christmas tree makes a thoughtful pre-holiday gift for anyone with limited space.

WHAT YOU NEED

Scissors
4-inch-tall, 6-inch-diameter silver bucket
Florist's foam
Hot-glue gun; hot-glue sticks
10-inch length of 1¾-inch-diameter tree branch
12-inch-tall plastic-foam cone
Bun moss
Thirty 1-inch-diameter silver ornaments
Green sheet moss
2 yards of 1½-inch-wide silver wire-edge ribbon

HERE'S HOW

1 Cut a block of florist's foam to fill bucket. Hot-glue the foam to the inside bottom of the bucket. Insert one end of the tree branch centered in the plastic-foam cone. Insert the opposite end into the center of the florist's foam in the bucket. Adjust the depth of branch until a trunk space of 4 inches remains between bucket and cone. Remove branch and place glue on both ends; reinsert into holes in foam; let dry.

2 Cut the bun moss into small, round pieces. Hot-glue the bun moss pieces to cone, covering it completely. Decorate the tree by gluing silver ornaments to sides and top. Cover exposed florist's foam in bucket with green sheet moss; hot-glue in place. Tie silver ribbon into a bow and glue it to sheet moss.

Natural Influence

This wreath has natural appeal for the holidays. Combine purchased and found natural items for one-of-a-kind front-door accents.

WHAT YOU NEED

Plastic-foam wreath base, such as Styrofoam
Hot-glue gun; hot-glue sticks
Thin sheets of birch bark
Purchased balls of grapevine, birch, and branch shavings
Pinecones
Pomegranates
Fresh or artificial greens
Floral pins, optional
Gold ribbon
Scissors
Rope garland
Miniature ornaments

HERE'S HOW

1 Hot-glue thin sheets of birch bark around the plastic-foam wreath base to cover.

2 Arrange and glue balls, pinecones, pomegranates, and fresh greens on bark-covered wreath. If working with fresh greens, use floral pins to attach so they may be removed before storing the wreath.

3 Tie two generous-size ribbon bows. Hot-glue in place. Wind rope garland through wreath, hot-gluing in spots to secure. Add miniature ornaments as desired.

Cookies, Cookies & More Cookies

"The black stove, stoked with coal and firewood, glows like a lighted pumpkin. Eggbeaters whirl, spoons spin round in bowls of butter and sugar, vanilla sweetens the air, ginger spices it; melting, nose-tingling odors saturate the kitchen, suffuse the house, drift out to the world on puffs of chimney smoke."

—Truman Capote

*This lemon-
and almond-
infused pastry
is sure to create
lasting
memories. Look
for shell-shape
madeleine pans
at kitchen
specialty shops.*

Delectable Duo

Lemony Nut Madeleines

WHAT YOU NEED

- ½ cup granulated sugar
- 2 egg yolks
- ½ cup butter (no substitutes), melted and cooled
- ½ teaspoon finely shredded lemon peel
- 1 tablespoon lemon juice
- ½ teaspoon vanilla
- ½ cup all-purpose flour
- ½ teaspoon baking powder
- ⅛ teaspoon baking soda
- ⅛ teaspoon salt
- ¼ cup finely chopped toasted almonds
- 2 slightly beaten egg whites
  Powdered sugar

HERE'S HOW

1 Preheat oven to 375°F. Grease and flour twenty-four 3-inch shell-shape madeleine molds. Set aside.

2 Beat granulated sugar and yolks in a medium mixing bowl with an electric mixer on medium to high speed for 30 seconds. Add butter, lemon peel, lemon juice, and vanilla. Beat on low speed until combined.

3 Sift together flour, baking powder, baking soda, and salt in a bowl. Sift or sprinkle flour mixture over the egg yolk mixture; gently fold in. Fold in almonds. Gently stir in egg whites. Spoon batter into prepared molds, filling each about half full.

4 Bake in preheated oven for 10 to 12 minutes or until edges are golden and tops spring back when lightly touched. Cool in molds for 1 minute. Using the point of a knife, loosen cookies from molds; invert onto a wire rack. Remove molds and cool cookies completely on rack.

5 Cover tightly and store at room temperature for up to 3 days. To serve, sift powdered sugar over tops of cookies. Makes 24.

Almond-Butter Crisps

In these delicate cookies, a sprinkling of ground almonds adds richness, egg-wash topping adds shine, and a candy coating adds a dainty decoration.

WHAT YOU NEED

1 cup butter (no substitutes)
1 cup sugar
2 cups all-purpose flour
1/2 cup blanched almonds, very finely ground
1 tablespoon finely shredded lemon peel
1 beaten egg
1 teaspoon water
5 ounces green candy coating, melted
5 ounces vanilla-flavor candy coating, melted

HERE'S HOW

1 Beat butter in a medium mixing bowl with an electric mixer on medium to high speed for 30 seconds. Add sugar and beat until combined, scraping sides of bowl occasionally. Beat in flour until combined. Stir in almonds and lemon peel. Divide dough into thirds. Cover and chill 1 hour.

2 Preheat oven to 350°F. Roll each portion of dough on a lightly floured surface to 1/8- to 1/4-inch thickness. Cut dough into shapes with floured 2 1/2-inch cookie cutters. Place cutouts 1 inch apart on an ungreased cookie sheet. Mix egg and water; brush over tops of cookies.

3 Bake in preheated oven for 8 to 10 minutes or until lightly golden. Cool on cookie sheet for 2 minutes. Transfer to wire racks and cool completely.

4 For frosting, dip half of each cookie into either green or white melted candy coating. Dot with some of the other color candy coating. Drag a toothpick through coatings to make a design. Let cookies stand on wire rack until coating is set. Makes about 60.

Creamy Lime Tartlets

WHAT YOU NEED

Sweet Tart Pastry
1/3 cup sugar
2 teaspoons cornstarch
1/3 cup whipping cream
1 teaspoon finely shredded lime peel
2 tablespoons lime juice
1 tablespoon butter or margarine
1/4 cup dairy sour cream
Green and yellow food coloring
Whipped cream
Finely shredded lime peel (optional)

Fill rich, buttery pastry shells with tart lime filling for lovely contrasting flavors.

HERE'S HOW

1 Preheat oven to 400°F. For shells, shape Sweet Tart Pastry into eighteen ¾-inch balls. Press balls into ungreased 1¾-inch muffin cups, pressing an even layer onto the bottom and up the sides of each cup. Bake in preheated oven for 8 to 10 minutes or until edges are lightly browned. Cool shells in muffin cups on wire racks for 10 minutes. Remove shells from cups and set aside to cool.

2 Meanwhile, for filling, combine sugar and cornstarch in a saucepan. Stir in whipping cream, the 1 teaspoon lime peel, and lime juice. Bring to boiling over medium-high heat, stirring constantly. Reduce heat; simmer for 1 minute, stirring constantly until thickened and smooth. Remove from heat. Stir in butter, sour cream, and enough food coloring to make a pale green mixture. Cool mixture to room temperature. Spoon into tart shells. Cover and chill for 2 to 4 hours.

3 To serve, spoon whipped cream onto each tartlet. If desired, top with shredded lime peel. Makes 18 tartlets.

4 **SWEET TART PASTRY:** Stir together ⅔ cup all-purpose flour and 2 tablespoons sugar in a bowl. Cut in ¼ cup cold butter until pieces are the size of small peas. Stir together 1 beaten egg yolk and 1½ teaspoons water in a small bowl; stir into flour mixture. Knead the dough just until a ball forms. If necessary, cover with plastic wrap and chill for 30 to 60 minutes or until dough is easy to handle.

Cookie Cutups

This holiday season, remember the people who make your life better with a gift from your heart and hearth—cutout cookies. Pack a basket of Christmas cheer with Citrus-Sour Cream Cutouts and Brown Sugar Cutouts.

Citrus-Sour Cream Cutouts

WHAT YOU NEED

- 1/2 cup butter (no substitutes)
- 1/3 cup shortening
- 1 cup sugar
- 3/4 teaspoon baking powder
- 1/2 teaspoon ground mace
- 1/4 teaspoon baking soda
- Dash salt
- 1/3 cup dairy sour cream
- 1 egg
- 1 teaspoon vanilla
- 2 1/2 cups all-purpose flour
- 1 teaspoon finely shredded lemon peel
- Royal Icing (recipe, page 288)
- Decorative candies, optional

HERE'S HOW

1 Beat butter and shortening in a large mixing bowl with an electric mixer on medium to high speed for 30 seconds. Add sugar, baking powder, mace, baking soda, and salt. Beat until combined, scraping sides of bowl occasionally. Beat in sour cream, egg, and vanilla. Beat in as much flour as you can with the mixer. Stir in remaining flour and lemon peel with a wooden spoon. Divide dough in half. Cover and chill for 1 to 2 hours or until easy to handle. (Or wrap in foil and freeze for up to 3 months. Thaw in refrigerator.)

2 Preheat oven to 375°F. Roll each half of the dough 1/8 to 1/4 inch thick on a well-floured pastry cloth. Keep remaining portion chilled. Cut into shapes with 2- to 2 1/2-inch cookie cutters dipped in flour. Place cutouts 1/2 inch apart on ungreased cookie sheets.

3 Bake in preheated oven for 7 to 8 minutes or until edges are firm and bottoms are very lightly browned. Cool on wire racks. Decorate with Royal Icing and decorative candies. Makes about 48.

Brown Sugar Cutouts

What You Need

1/3 cup **butter or margarine**
1/3 cup **shortening**
3/4 cup **packed brown sugar**
1 teaspoon **baking powder**
1/2 teaspoon **ground cinnamon**
1/4 teaspoon **salt**
1 teaspoon **instant coffee crystals**
1 **egg**
1/2 teaspoon **vanilla**
1 3/4 cups **all-purpose flour**
1/4 cup **whole wheat flour**
Royal Icing (recipe, page 288) (optional)

Here's How

1 Beat butter and shortening in a large mixing bowl with
an electric mixer on medium to high speed for 30 seconds.
Add brown sugar, baking powder, cinnamon, and salt;
beat until combined. Dissolve instant coffee crystals in
1 tablespoon warm water. Beat coffee mixture, egg, and
vanilla into sugar mixture. Beat in as much of the
all-purpose flour as you can with the mixer. Stir in
remaining all-purpose flour and whole wheat flour with
a wooden spoon. Divide dough in half. Cover and chill
about 3 hours or until easy to handle.

2 Preheat oven to 375°F. Roll each half of dough 1/8 inch
thick on a lightly floured surface. Cut into shapes with
2- to 2 1/2-inch cookie cutters dipped in flour. Place cutouts
1 inch apart on ungreased cookie sheets.

3 Bake in preheated oven for 7 to 8 minutes or until edges
are firm. Cool on cookie sheet for 1 minute. Remove and
cool on wire racks. If desired, decorate with Royal Icing.
Makes about 40.

A little lemon peel adds distinction to rich, light-color Citrus-Sour Cream Cutout. The Brown Sugar Cutouts recipe is the perfect texture and color for cutting crisp gingerbread boys and girls.

43

Songbird Cookies

Wearing bright plumage, a bluebird and a cardinal share a nest with a flock of other colorful Songbird Cookies.

WHAT YOU NEED

- $1/2$ **cup butter or margarine**
- $1/3$ **cup shortening**
- $1/3$ **cup sugar**
- $1^1/2$ **teaspoons baking powder**
- 1 **egg**
- $1/3$ **cup dairy sour cream**
- $2^3/4$ **cups all-purpose flour**
- 2 **teaspoons finely shredded orange peel**
- **Songbird Frosting**

HERE'S HOW

1 Beat butter and shortening in a large mixing bowl with an electric mixer on medium to high speed for 30 seconds. Add sugar and baking powder; beat until combined. Beat in egg and sour cream. Beat in as much flour as you can with the mixer. Stir in orange peel and any remaining flour with a wooden spoon. Divide dough in half. Cover and chill for 2 hours or until easy to handle.

2 Preheat oven to 375°F. Roll each half of dough ⅛ inch thick on a lightly floured surface. Cut with desired bird-shape cookie cutters. Place cutouts on an ungreased cookie sheet.

3 Bake in preheated oven for 5 to 6 minutes or until edges are firm and bottoms are very lightly browned. Cool on wire racks. Decorate with Songbird Frosting. Makes about 96.

4 **SONGBIRD FROSTING:** Combine ½ cup water, 3 tablespoons light corn syrup, and 1 tablespoon shortening in a small saucepan; cook and stir just until warm. Transfer to a bowl. Add one 2-pound package sifted powdered sugar; beat with an electric mixer on low speed until combined. Add water, 1 teaspoon at a time, beating at high speed until frosting is smooth and spreadable. Divide into portions, one portion for each color you plan to use. Color as desired with paste food coloring. Keep frosting covered when not in use. Makes 3 cups.

Holiday Toffee Cakes

An elegant chocolate drizzle patterns a plate of Holiday Toffee Cakes, accenting rich English-toffee flavor.

WHAT YOU NEED

2 1.4-ounce packages chocolate-covered toffee pieces (¹/₂ cup)
³/₄ cup butter or margarine
¹/₃ cup sugar
1 tablespoon milk
2 teaspoons vanilla
2³/₄ cups all-purpose flour
¹/₂ cup semisweet chocolate pieces
2 teaspoons shortening

HERE'S HOW

1 Finely chop chocolate-covered toffee pieces. Set aside.

2 Beat butter in a large mixing bowl with an electric mixer on medium to high speed for 30 seconds. Add sugar; beat until combined. Beat in milk and vanilla. Beat in as much flour as you can with the mixer. Stir in remaining flour and the chopped chocolate-covered toffee pieces with a wooden spoon, if necessary. Cover and chill 1 hour or until easy to handle.

3 Preheat oven to 325°F. Shape dough into 1-inch balls. Place 1 inch apart on ungreased cookie sheets. Bake in a preheated oven for 15 to 20 minutes or until bottoms are lightly browned. Cool on wire racks.

4 Combine chocolate pieces and shortening in a small saucepan over low heat. Heat and stir just until chocolate is melted. Drizzle over cookies on plate. Makes about 45.

Christmas Flowers

It's a blooming wonder how this pliable dough can be molded into such Christmas Flowers as poinsettias, tulips, and roses.

WHAT YOU NEED

3/4 cup butter or margarine
2/3 cup shortening
1 1/2 cups sugar
1 tablespoon baking powder
1/4 teaspoon salt
2 eggs
1 teaspoon vanilla
4 cups all-purpose flour
Paste or liquid food coloring

HERE'S HOW

1 Beat butter or margarine and shortening in a large mixing bowl with an electric mixer on medium to high speed for 30 seconds. Add sugar, baking powder, and salt; beat until combined. Beat in eggs and vanilla until combined. Beat in as much flour as you can with the mixer. Stir in any remaining flour with a wooden spoon (dough should be stiff). Cover and chill dough at least 2 hours or overnight.

2 Preheat oven to 300°F. Divide dough into portions, one for each color. Knead food coloring into each portion, adding it slowly until dough is desired color (colors lighten slightly when dough is baked).

3 Break off small pieces of different colors of dough and form into flower shapes. Place flowers 2 inches apart on ungreased cookie sheets.

4 Bake in the preheated oven for 15 minutes or until edges are firm and cookies look set and bottoms are not brown. Cool on wire racks. Makes about 24.

Soft Ginger Cookies

Santa would love to find this delicious stack of cookies beside his glass of milk on Christmas Eve. Because the recipe makes at least three dozen cookies, there will be some left over for his elves.

WHAT YOU NEED

2$^1/_4$ cups all-purpose flour
  2 teaspoons ground ginger
  1 teaspoon baking soda
$^3/_4$ teaspoon ground cinnamon
$^1/_2$ teaspoon ground cloves
$^1/_4$ teaspoon salt
$^3/_4$ cup butter (no substitutes), softened
  1 cup sugar
  1 egg
$^1/_4$ cup molasses
  2 tablespoons sugar

HERE'S HOW

1 Preheat oven to 350°F. Combine flour, ginger, baking soda, cinnamon, cloves, and salt. Set aside. In a large mixing bowl with an electric mixer beat butter for 30 seconds. Add 1 cup sugar. Beat until fluffy.

2 Add egg and molasses; beat well. Add half the flour mixture; beat until combined. Stir in remaining flour with a wooden spoon.

3 Shape into 1-inch balls. Roll in 2 tablespoons sugar; place on ungreased cookie sheets 2 inches apart. Bake in the preheated oven 10 minutes or until light brown and puffed. Let cool on cookie sheets 2 minutes. Transfer to wire racks to cool. Makes about 36 cookies.

Frosty Snowballs

WHAT YOU NEED

   1 **cup butter (no substitutes), softened**

  1/3 **cup granulated sugar**

   1 **tablespoon water**

   1 **teaspoon vanilla**

2¼ **cups all-purpose flour**

   1 **cup chopped pecans**

    Green, pink, and purple edible cake sparkles or colored sugar

   1 **cup sifted powdered sugar**

HERE'S HOW

1 Preheat oven to 325°F. Beat butter in a large mixing bowl with an electric mixer on medium speed for 30 seconds. Add the granulated sugar. Beat until combined, scraping bowl. Beat in water and vanilla until combined. Beat in as much of the flour as you can with the mixer. Stir in the remaining flour and the chopped pecans.

2 Shape dough into 1-inch balls. Place 1 inch apart on ungreased cookie sheets. Bake in the preheated oven for about 20 minutes or until bottoms are lightly browned. Transfer cookies to wire racks to cool.

3 Place one color of edible cake sparkles or colored sugar in each of three small bowls. To each bowl, add ⅓ cup of the sifted powdered sugar; mix together. Gently roll and shake cooled cookies in powdered sugar mixture. Makes about 36.

Place colorful shimmer in a holiday cookie tin with these bite-size sugared snowballs. With the variety of colored sparkles and sugar available, you can make these cookies any color.

$\mathscr{S}$ugar & $\mathscr{S}$pice $\mathscr{B}$ars

Whether your family loves chocolate, nuts, raspberries, or spice, this tasty quartet of bars offers everyone a favorite. The Raspberry-Almond Ribbons, shown beneath the serving plate, opposite, are topped with jam, almonds, and a drizzling of icing.

Raspberry-Almond Ribbons

WHAT YOU NEED

1¾ cups all-purpose flour
2 teaspoons baking powder
¼ teaspoon salt
½ cup butter (no substitutes), softened
1 cup granulated sugar
1 egg
¼ teaspoon almond extract
½ cup seedless raspberry jam
½ cup toasted chopped almonds
1 cup sifted powdered sugar
¼ teaspoon vanilla
2–3 tablespoons milk

HERE'S HOW

1 Preheat oven to 325°F. Combine flour, baking powder, and salt; set aside. In a large bowl beat butter 30 seconds. Add granulated sugar and beat until fluffy. Add egg and almond extract. Beat well. Beat in half flour mixture until combined. Stir in remaining flour mixture with wooden spoon. Divide dough into fourths. Shape each portion into a 13×2-inch rectangle; place 4 to 5 inches apart on 2 ungreased baking sheets. Bake in oven 12 to 14 minutes or until edges are firm. Cool on cookie sheets 2 minutes; transfer to wire rack to cool.

2 Spread 2 tablespoons jam along center of each bar. Sprinkle almonds along sides of each bar next to jam. Stir together powdered sugar, vanilla, and enough milk to make a drizzling consistency. Drizzle over bars. Cut into 1-inch-thick slices. Makes about 52.

Sugar & Spice Bars recipes continued on pages 56–57

Sugar & Spice Bars

These delicious bars are brushed with Lemon Icing and topped with candied fruits.

Pan Lebkuchen

WHAT YOU NEED

- 2 cups all-purpose flour
- 1 tablespoon pumpkin pie spice
- ½ teaspoon baking soda
- 1 egg
- 2 tablespoons cooking oil
- ½ cup packed brown sugar
- ⅓ cup honey
- ⅓ cup dark molasses
- ½ cup chopped almonds
- ½ cup diced mixed candied fruits and peels, finely chopped
  Lemon Icing

HERE'S HOW

1 Preheat oven to 350°F. Stir together flour, pumpkin pie spice, and baking soda. In a large bowl beat together egg and oil. Add brown sugar and beat until fluffy. Stir in honey and molasses. Add flour mixture and beat until well mixed. Stir in almonds and ½ cup diced candied fruits and peels.

2 Spread in greased 15×10×1-inch baking pan. Bake in the preheated oven 15 minutes or until toothpick inserted near center comes out clean. Immediately score into 48 bars with sharp knife. Brush with Lemon Icing. Garnish with additional candied fruits, if desired. Makes 48 bars.

3 LEMON ICING: In a bowl beat together 1½ cups sifted powdered sugar, ½ teaspoon finely shredded lemon peel, and 1 tablespoon or more lemon juice until smooth.

Chopped walnuts or pecans add a nutty treat in every bite of these fudge brownies.

Fudgy Brownies

WHAT YOU NEED

- 4 ounces unsweetened chocolate, chopped
- ½ cup butter
- 1 cup all-purpose flour
- ¾ cup chopped toasted walnuts or toasted pecans

¼ teaspoon baking powder
1½ cups sugar
 3 eggs, slightly beaten
 1 teaspoon vanilla
   Chocolate-Sour Cream Frosting

HERE'S HOW

1 Preheat oven to 350°F. Grease and lightly flour 8×8×2-inch baking pan; set aside. Melt chocolate and butter in saucepan over low heat, stirring occasionally; set aside. In a bowl stir together flour, nuts, and baking powder; set aside.

2 In a large bowl, stir together melted chocolate mixture and sugar. Add eggs and vanilla. Using a wooden spoon, lightly beat until just combined. Stir in flour mixture. Spread batter in prepared pan. Bake in the preheated oven for 50 minutes for 8×8×2-inch pan or 40 minutes for 9×9×2-inch pan. Cool in pan on wire rack. Frost with Chocolate-Sour Cream Frosting; refrigerate. Cut into bars. Makes 12 to 16.

3 **Chocolate-Sour Cream Frosting**: In a saucepan melt ½ cup semisweet chocolate pieces and 2 tablespoons butter over low heat; stir frequently. Cool 5 minutes. Stir in ½ cup sour cream. Add 1¼ cups powdered sugar. Beat until smooth.

Cashew Squares

WHAT YOU NEED

¼ cup butter
1 cup all-purpose flour
1 cup packed brown sugar
1 egg, slightly beaten
1 teaspoon baking powder
2 tablespoons milk
½ teaspoon vanilla
1 cup coarsely chopped cashews or mixed nuts
  Powdered sugar

HERE'S HOW

1 Preheat oven to 350°F. In a saucepan melt butter; remove from heat. Add remaining ingredients, except powdered sugar. Spread in greased 8×8×2-inch baking pan. Bake in preheated oven 20 minutes or until toothpick inserted in center comes out clean. Cool slightly in pan on wire rack. Cut into bars; cool in pan. Sprinkle bars with powdered sugar. Makes 16.

Because they require just a handful of ingredients, these delicious bars can be made in minutes to offer to family and holiday visitors.

Honey-Nut Wedges

WHAT YOU NEED

- 1 15-ounce package folded, refrigerated, unbaked piecrust (2 crusts)
- 1¼ cups finely chopped walnuts
- ⅓ cup sugar
- 3 tablespoons honey
- 1 teaspoon lemon juice
- 1 teaspoon ground cinnamon
- Milk
- Additional sugar
- Ground cinnamon

HERE'S HOW

1 Preheat oven to 375°F. Let pastry stand at room temperature for 15 minutes. On a floured surface, roll out one of the piecrusts to a 12-inch circle. Transfer crust to a large ungreased cookie sheet. Roll out remaining piecrust to a 12-inch circle; set aside.

2 For filling, combine walnuts, ⅓ cup sugar, honey, lemon juice, and 1 teaspoon cinnamon in a small mixing bowl. Spread filling to within ½ inch of the edge of the piecrust on the cookie sheet.

3 Prick top or cut small shapes from remaining crust. Place the crust on the filling and moisten edges with water to seal. Crimp edges. Brush with milk and sprinkle with additional sugar and cinnamon.

4 Bake in the preheated oven for 18 to 20 minutes or until golden brown. If necessary to prevent overbrowning, cover edges of pastry with foil during the last 5 minutes of baking time. Cool for 10 minutes on a wire rack. While warm, cut into 16 wedges. Cool completely on a wire rack. Makes 16 wedges.

Walnuts lend a distinctive flavor to the filling in these golden wedges.

Big Batch Bars

Super-Easy Chocolate Bars

WHAT YOU NEED

  1 cup butter (no substitutes)
  ½ cup sugar
  ⅛ teaspoon salt
  2 cups all-purpose flour
  1 14-ounce can (1¼ cups) sweetened condensed milk
  1 cup (½ of a 12-ounce package) semisweet
     chocolate pieces
  ½ cup chopped walnuts or pecans
  ½ teaspoon vanilla

HERE'S HOW

1 Preheat oven to 350°F. For crust, beat butter in a large
   mixing bowl with an electric mixer on medium to high
   speed for 30 seconds. Add sugar and salt; beat until
   combined, scraping sides of bowl occasionally. Beat in the
   flour on low speed until combined. Press two-thirds of the
   crust mixture into the bottom of an ungreased
   13×9×2-inch baking pan.

2 For filling, combine sweetened condensed milk and
   chocolate in a medium saucepan. Stir over low heat until
   chocolate melts and mixture is smooth. Remove from heat.
   Stir in nuts and vanilla. Spread hot mixture over the crust.
   Dot with remaining crust mixture.

3 Bake in the preheated oven about 35 minutes or until
   golden. Cool in pan on a wire rack. To ensure even
   squares, cool the layered bars thoroughly before cutting so
   they have time to set up. Cut into squares. Makes about
   25 bars.

Clockwise from left, Super-Easy Chocolate Bars, Apricot-Nut Diamonds, and Cranberry-Macadamia Bars are sweet solutions when you don't have time to shape and bake individual cookies.

Big Batch Bars recipes are continued on pages 62–63.

Powdered Sugar Icing adds a pretty and sweet coat to the top of these irresistible holiday bars.

Apricot-Nut Diamonds

WHAT YOU NEED

1 cup all-purpose flour
Dash salt
¼ cup butter (no substitutes)
½ cup snipped dried apricots
¾ cup packed brown sugar
2 eggs
1 cup chopped walnuts
½ cup coconut
1 teaspoon vanilla
2 tablespoons all-purpose flour
Powdered Sugar Icing

HERE'S HOW

1 Preheat oven to 375°F. For crust, combine the 1 cup flour and salt in a mixing bowl. Cut in butter until crumbly. Press into the bottom of a lightly greased 11×7×1½-inch baking pan. Bake in the preheated oven for 12 minutes.

2 Meanwhile, combine apricots and enough water to cover in a small saucepan. Bring to boiling. Reduce heat and simmer, covered, for 10 minutes; drain.

3 For topping, stir together brown sugar and eggs in a large mixing bowl until combined. Stir in drained apricots, walnuts, coconut, and vanilla. Add the 2 tablespoons flour; stir until combined. Spread mixture evenly over crust.

4 Bake in the preheated oven for 15 minutes. Cool in pan on a wire rack. Drizzle with Powdered Sugar Icing. Cut into diamonds: Cut straight lines along the length of the pan. Cut diagonal lines across the pan. Trim the end pieces into triangles, rectangles, or squares. Cover and store in the refrigerator. Makes about 30 bars.

5 **POWDERED SUGAR ICING:** Stir together 1 cup sifted powdered sugar, ¼ teaspoon vanilla, and 1 tablespoon milk in a small bowl. Stir in additional milk, 1 teaspoon at a time, until icing is smooth and of drizzling consistency.

Cranberry-Macadamia Bars

WHAT YOU NEED

- 1¼ cups all-purpose flour
- ¾ cup sugar
- ½ cup butter (no substitutes)
- 1 cup finely chopped macadamia nuts, hazelnuts (filberts), or pecans
- 1¼ cups sugar
- 2 beaten eggs
- 2 tablespoons milk
- 1 teaspoon finely shredded orange peel
- 1 teaspoon vanilla
- 1 cup finely chopped cranberries
- ½ cup coconut

HERE'S HOW

1 Preheat oven to 350°F. For crust, stir together flour and the ¾ cup sugar in a medium mixing bowl. Cut in butter until mixture resembles coarse crumbs. Stir in ½ cup of the nuts. Press the flour mixture into the bottom of an ungreased 13×9×2-inch baking pan.

2 Bake in the preheated oven for 10 to 15 minutes or until the crust is light brown around the edges.

3 Meanwhile, for topping, combine the 1¼ cups sugar, the eggs, milk, orange peel, and vanilla. Beat until combined. Pour over the hot crust. Sprinkle with the remaining nuts, cranberries, and coconut.

4 Bake in the preheated oven for 30 minutes or until golden. Cool slightly in pan on a wire rack. Cut into rectangles while warm. Cool completely. Makes 24 bars.

A nutty crust makes a delicious base for this cranberry-flavored bar. Topped with coconut and chopped nuts, this colorful holiday dessert will disappear as quickly as a snowflake in your hand.

Tasty-Stack Cookies

One dough with a few magical variations can create two different cookies—Lemon-Almond Cookies and Santa's Whiskers—for your holiday platter. Chilling the dough for the cherry-and-coconut-flavored cookies makes it easier to slice.

Tasty-Stack Cookie Dough

WHAT YOU NEED

$^3/_4$ cup butter (no substitutes), softened
$^3/_4$ cup shortening
$1^1/_2$ cups sugar
$^1/_4$ teaspoon baking soda
$^1/_4$ teaspoon salt
 1 egg
 1 egg yolk
 3 tablespoons milk
$1^1/_2$ teaspoons vanilla
$4^1/_2$ cups all-purpose flour

HERE'S HOW

1 Place butter and shortening in a large bowl; beat with a mixer on medium to high speed 30 seconds. Add sugar, baking soda, and salt. Beat until combined, scraping sides of bowl occasionally. Beat in the egg, egg yolk, milk, and vanilla. Beat in as much of the flour as possible with the mixer. Using a wooden spoon, stir in any remaining flour. Divide cookie dough into three equal portions for the desired recipes below and opposite.

Lemon-Almond Cookie Variation

WHAT YOU NEED

$^1/_3$ recipe Tasty-Stack Cookie Dough
 2 teaspoons finely shredded lemon peel
 1 teaspoon almond extract
   Lemon Frosting
$^1/_2$ cup sliced almonds, toasted

HERE'S HOW

1 Combine the cookie dough, lemon peel, and almond extract in a bowl. Using a wooden spoon, mix thoroughly.

2 Shape dough into an 8-inch-long roll. Wrap in plastic wrap or waxed paper. Chill in the refrigerator at least 4 hours.

3 Preheat oven to 375°F. Using a sharp knife, cut dough into ¼-inch-thick slices. Place slices 2 inches apart on an ungreased cookie sheet. Bake for 8 to 10 minutes or until edges are firm and bottoms are lightly browned. Transfer cookies to a wire rack; cool.

4 Spread about 1 teaspoon of Lemon Frosting on each cookie. Sprinkle with toasted sliced almonds. Makes 32 cookies.

5 LEMON FROSTING: Place ¼ cup butter, softened, in a bowl. Beat butter with a mixer on medium to high speed about 30 seconds. Gradually add 1 cup sifted powdered sugar, beating until combined. Beat in 4 teaspoons milk, 1 teaspoon lemon juice, ¼ teaspoon vanilla, a few drops almond extract, and a few drops of yellow food coloring. Beat in 1 cup sifted powdered sugar until smooth.

Santa's Whiskers Variation

WHAT YOU NEED

³⁄₄ **cup maraschino cherries, drained and finely chopped**
¹⁄₃ **recipe Tasty-Stack Cookie Dough**
     Few drops red food coloring
¹⁄₂ **cup coconut**

HERE'S HOW

1 Pat cherries dry; combine with cookie dough and food coloring in a bowl. Using a wooden spoon, mix thoroughly.

2 Shape dough into a 10-inch-long roll. Roll dough in coconut until covered. Wrap in plastic wrap or waxed paper. Chill in refrigerator at least 4 hours or until firm.

3 Preheat oven to 375°F. Cut dough into ¼-inch-thick slices. Place slices 2 inches apart on an ungreased cookie sheet.

4 Bake in the preheated oven for 8 to 10 minutes or until edges are firm and bottoms are lightly browned. Transfer cookies to a wire rack; cool. Makes about 36 cookies.

Candy Striped

For extra sweetness, drizzle a spoonful of melted candy coating over these yummy treats.

Lemon-Molasses Squares

WHAT YOU NEED

$1/2$	cup butter (no substitutes)
1	cup sugar
1	teaspoon ground cinnamon
$1/2$	teaspoon baking soda
$1/4$	teaspoon salt
$1/4$	cup molasses
1	egg
$2^1/4$	cups all-purpose flour
3	slightly beaten egg yolks
$1/4$	cup lemon juice
1	cup flaked coconut
1	tablespoon finely shredded lemon peel
3	ounces white baking bar

HERE'S HOW

1 Beat butter in a large bowl with an electric mixer on medium speed for 30 seconds. Add sugar, cinnamon, baking soda, and salt; beat until combined. Beat in molasses and egg until combined. Beat in as much flour as you can with the mixer. Stir in any remaining flour with a wooden spoon. Divide dough in half; cover and chill until easy to handle.

2 For filling, combine egg yolks, lemon juice, ⅛ teaspoon *salt*, and 1 tablespoon water in a small saucepan. Cook and stir over medium heat until thickened and bubbly. Cook and stir 1 minute more. Stir in coconut and lemon peel. Cool.

3 Preheat oven to 350°F. Roll each portion of dough on a lightly floured surface into a 15×6-inch rectangle. Cut in half lengthwise, making two 15×3-inch rectangles. Spread a fourth of the filling in a 1-inch-wide strip along the center of each rectangle. Fold long sides over filling, overlapping slightly in center; seal. Place seam side down; flatten slightly. Cut crosswise into 1½-inch bars. Place bars 1½ inches apart on ungreased cookie sheets. Bake in oven for 12 minutes or until set. Cool on wire racks. Drizzle with melted candy coating. Makes 40 cookies.

Raspberry Cookies

WHAT YOU NEED

8 ounces white
    baking bar
$^1/_2$ cup butter
1 cup sugar
1 teaspoon baking soda
$^1/_4$ teaspoon salt
2 eggs
$2^3/_4$ cups all-purpose flour
$^1/_2$ cup seedless
    raspberry jam
3 ounces white
    baking bar
$^1/_2$ teaspoon shortening

HERE'S HOW

1 Preheat oven to 375°F.
Chop 4 ounces of the white baking bar; set aside. In a small
heavy saucepan melt the remaining 4 ounces white baking bar
over low heat, stirring constantly. Remove from heat; cool.

2 In a large mixing bowl beat butter with an electric mixer
on medium to high speed 30 seconds or until softened.
Add sugar, baking soda, and salt. Beat until combined.
Beat in eggs and melted baking bar until combined. Beat
in as much flour as you can. Stir in remaining flour with a
wooden spoon. Stir in chopped baking bar. Drop by
rounded teaspoonfuls 2 inches apart onto a greased cookie
sheet. Bake in the preheated oven for 7 to 9 minutes or
until light brown around edges. Cool on cookie sheet
1 minute. Remove and cool on a wire rack.

3 Before serving, melt jam in a small saucepan over low heat.
Spoon about $^1/_2$ teaspoon jam onto each cookie. In a small
heavy saucepan, combine the 3 ounces baking bar and the
shortening. Melt over low heat, stirring constantly. Drizzle
over cookies. If necessary, chill cookies about 15 minutes
to firm coating. Makes about 48 cookies.

Hazelnut Krinkle Cookies

WHAT YOU NEED

  3 cups all-purpose flour
  2 teaspoons baking powder
  1/2 teaspoon salt
  1 11-ounce jar chocolate-hazelnut spread
  1/4 cup shortening
  1 1/3 cups granulated sugar
  1 teaspoon vanilla
  2 eggs
  1/3 cup milk
  1/2 cup chopped, toasted hazelnuts
  2 cups finely chopped hazelnuts
  Sifted powdered sugar

HERE'S HOW

1 Preheat oven to 375°F. In a mixing bowl stir together flour, baking powder, and 1/2 teaspoon salt; set aside. In a large mixing bowl combine chocolate-hazelnut spread and shortening; beat with electric mixer on medium to high speed until combined. Add granulated sugar; beat on medium speed until fluffy. Add vanilla and eggs; beat until combined. Alternately add flour mixture and milk to creamed mixture, beating on medium speed just until combined. Stir in 1/2 cup chopped nuts. Chill, covered, several hours or until firm.

2 Shape dough into 1- or 1 1/2-inch balls. Roll balls in finely chopped nuts, then the powdered sugar. Place balls 2 inches apart on a lightly greased cookie sheet. (Cookies will spread and crinkle as they bake.) Bake in the preheated oven 8 to 10 minutes or until surface is cracked and cookies are set. Cool cookies on wire rack. Makes about 6 dozen small cookies.

The cracked surface of these chocolate-hazelnut cookies will tempt everyone to break them apart and eat them up.

Sugared Snowflakes

These spice-infused cookies should last the holiday season hanging indoors in a light-filled window or on the tree. A combination of cookie cutters and a drinking straw gives each cookie a one-of-a-kind pattern.

WHAT YOU NEED

- 2 **cups all-purpose flour**
- 1½ **teaspoons baking powder**
- ½ **teaspoon ground cinnamon**
- ¼ **teaspoon salt**
- ¼ **teaspoon ground nutmeg**
- ½ **cup butter or margarine**
- ¼ **cup shortening**
- ¾ **cup sugar**
- 1 **egg**
- 1 **tablespoon orange or lemon juice**

HERE'S HOW

1 In a mixing bowl combine flour, baking powder, cinnamon, salt, and nutmeg; set aside. In large mixing bowl beat butter and shortening 30 seconds to soften. Add sugar; beat until fluffy. Add egg and juice; beat well. Add flour mixture and beat or stir until well mixed. Divide in half. Chill, covered, 3 hours or until dough is easy to handle.

2 Preheat oven to 375°F. Roll dough on a lightly floured surface to ⅛-inch thickness. Cut with 2½-inch snowflake, star, or scalloped round cookie cutter. Using 2 sizes of drinking straws or aspic cutters, cut holes from cutouts, twisting straws slightly if necessary. Place cutouts on ungreased cookie sheet. Bake in the preheated oven 7 to 8 minutes or until edges are light brown. Remove and cool on wire rack. When cookies are cool, sift generously with powdered sugar. Makes about 36 cookies.

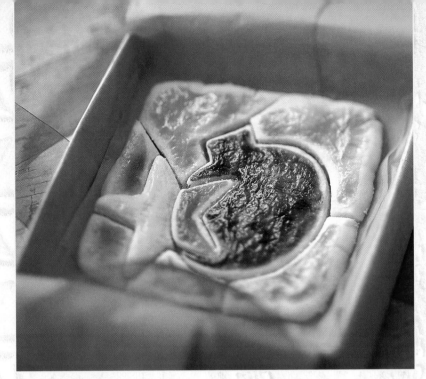

Puzzle Pieces

Children will be thrilled to make, give, and receive these puzzle cookies. A simple butter-cookie dough is cut with cutters, painted with thoroughly edible Egg-Yolk Paint, and then baked.

WHAT YOU NEED

1¼ cups all-purpose flour

3 tablespoons sugar

½ cup butter (no substitutes), slightly softened

  Egg-Yolk Paint

HERE'S HOW

1 Preheat oven to 325°F. In a mixing bowl combine flour and sugar. Cut in butter until mixture resembles fine crumbs and begins to cling. Form mixture into a ball and knead until mixture is smooth.

2 Divide dough into 6 portions. On ungreased cookie sheet, pat each portion into a 4-inch square. Press well-floured 2½-inch cookie cutter into center of square. Carefully remove cutter. Using a table knife, cut outside portion of square into large puzzle pieces. Brush cookie with different colors of Egg-Yolk Paint. Bake in the preheated oven 8 to 10 minutes or until bottoms start to brown and centers are set. While warm, recut pieces. Cool on wire rack.

3 **EGG-YOLK PAINT:** Beat 2 egg yolks and 2 teaspoons water in a small bowl. Divide among 3 or 4 small bowls. Add 2 or 3 drops food coloring to each bowl; mix well. Apply with a small, clean paintbrush. If paint thickens, stir in water, one drop at a time. Makes 6 cookies.

More Precious
To Give

"The joy of brightening other lives, bearing each other's burdens, easing others' loads and supplanting empty hearts and lives with generous gifts becomes for us the magic of Christmas."

—W. C. Jones

Christmas Music Caddy

WHAT YOU NEED

Black and white photocopies of Christmas sheet music
Decorative-edge scissors
Wood compact disc holder
Decoupage medium
Paintbrush
¼-inch-diameter red cord
Ruler
Hot-glue gun; hot-glue sticks
Medium-gauge silver wire
2 medium silver jingle bells
4 large silver jingle bells

HERE'S HOW

1 Trim the photocopies of sheet music using decorative-edge scissors as shown, *right*. Arrange sheet music on CD holder, trimming sheets as needed.

2 Paint the back of the sheets of music with decoupage medium. Position them on box, covering the sides and the top edges of the box. Coat with decoupage medium as shown, *right*. Let dry and coat with additional decoupage medium. Let dry.

3 Measure the top edges of the box. Add 10 inches to the measurement and cut cord to that length. Glue cord around the top edges of the box, leaving equal-length tails at one corner. Knot cord and glue in place.

4 Cut two 10-inch pieces of wire. Thread a medium jingle bell on each length. Twist once to secure the bell in the center of the wire. Tightly wrap the wires around the ends of the cord.

5 Glue a large jingle bell at each bottom corner of the box. Let dry.

Organize Christmas music in this decoupaged box that jingles all the way.

Merry Mittens

No one will mind bundling up for the cold with these delightful mittens to keep hands warm. Choose colorful taffeta with satin yo-yos or velvety swirls of rhinestones to make your winter wear special.

No one will mind bundling up for the cold with these delightful mittens to keep hands warm. Choose colorful taffeta with satin yo-yos or velvety swirls of rhinestones to make your winter wear special.

Velvet Swirl Mittens

WHAT YOU NEED

Tracing paper; pencil; scissors
½ yard each of velvet mitten and lining fabrics
Two 6½-inch squares of fleece for cuff
Stamp for fabric embossing
Press cloth; iron
20 inches of ¼-inch-wide elastic
60 small rhinestones for mittens
32 large rhinestones for cuffs
Fabric glue

HERE'S HOW

1 Test the fabric before beginning with mitten pieces. To emboss velvet, work on a firm, protected surface. Turn the stamp facing up. Place the mitten front right side down on the stamp. Place slightly damp press cloth on fabric and press with medium-hot iron (no steam) for 20 seconds. *Do not* slide or rock the iron, which may distort the embossing. Assemble the mittens as described on *page 78.* Glue on the rhinestone details.

Taffeta Yo-Yo Mittens

WHAT YOU NEED

Tracing paper; pencil; scissors
½ yard each of taffeta mitten and lining fabrics
Two 6½-inch squares of corduroy for cuff
Press cloth; iron
3¼-inch circles of satin
Buttons with openings through the top
¾ yard of ⅛-inch-wide green grosgrain ribbon for flower variation
20 inches of ¼-inch-wide elastic

Merry Mittens instructions are continued on pages 78–79.

76

Merry Mittens

1 For yo-yos, sew a running stitch around the edge of each satin circle. Pull threads to gather tightly. For the flower version, fold a 6-inch piece of ribbon into a stem shape. Make a ribbon-loop leaf approximately 2½ inches long. Topstitch in place. For yo-yos in a row, hand-stitch three yo-yos to each mitten front (after they are cut out). Sew a button to each center.

TO ASSEMBLE THE MITTENS

1 Enlarge and trace the mitten pattern, *opposite*, onto tracing paper and cut out. Cut shapes from mitten and lining fabrics (reversing pattern for one mitten).

2 Stitch mitten seams, right sides facing and sewing a ¼-inch seam allowance. Stitch the thumb gusset around the curved edge from A to B. Stitch the inner seam of thumb and palm, tapering to a point at A. Cut the elastic in half. Machine-zigzag over the elastic stretched on the wrong side of the palm/thumb, 3 inches from the top edge. Trim excess elastic.

3 Stitch mitten palm to back along side and finger curve. Turn right side out.

4 Repeat Steps 2 and 3 for the lining, leaving an opening for turning in side seam.

5 Stitch ends of each cuff together. Press seams open. Fold cuff in half, wrong sides facing and matching raw edges. Ease-stitch along the top edge of the cuff and baste to the mitten.

6 Slip mitten into lining, matching side seams and thumb. Stitch top edge. Slip-stitch opening in lining closed. Tuck the lining into mitten and turn cuff down.

YO-YO RUNNING STITCH

YO-YO AFTER GATHERING

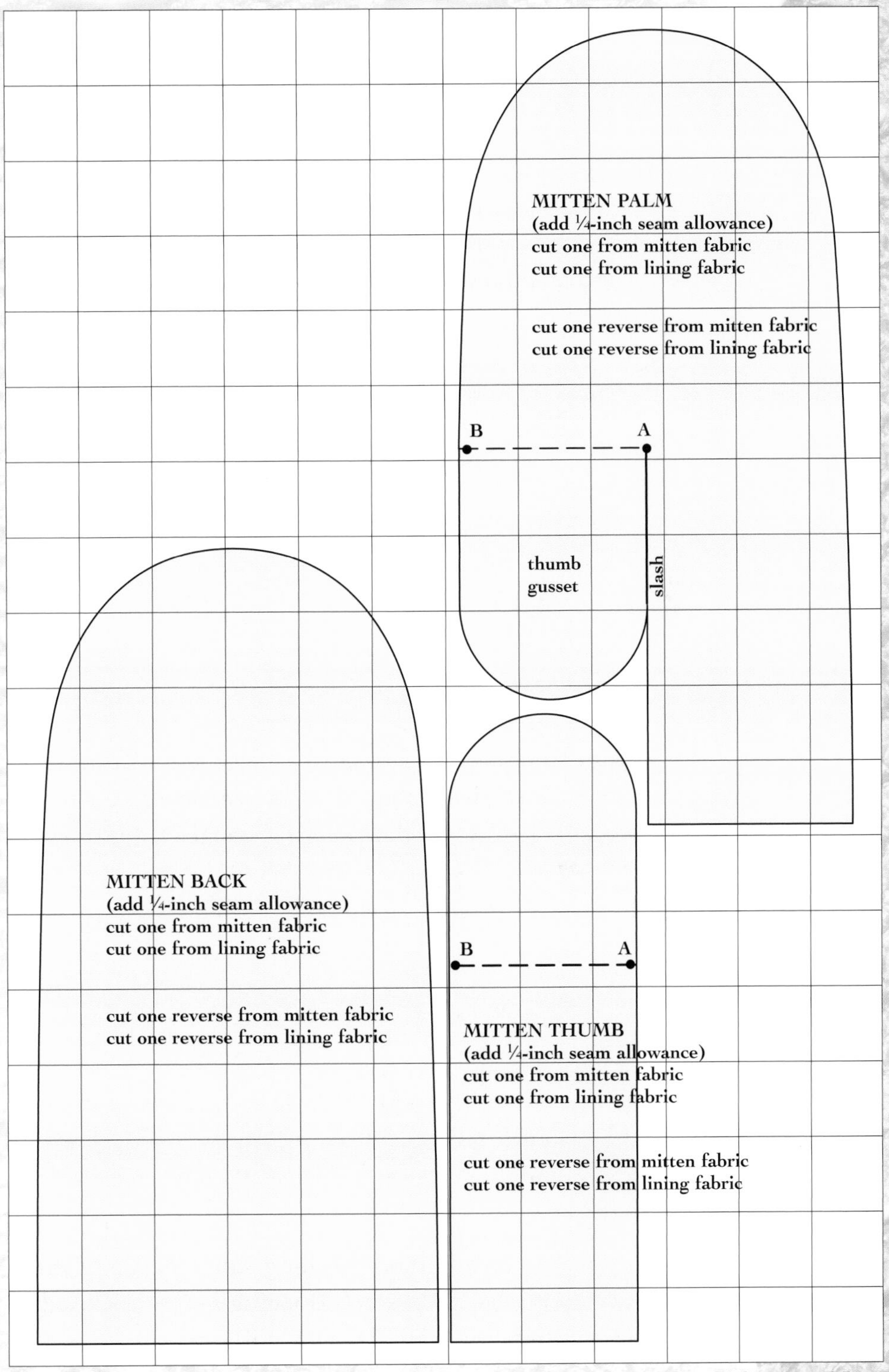

MITTEN PALM
(add ¼-inch seam allowance)
cut one from mitten fabric
cut one from lining fabric

cut one reverse from mitten fabric
cut one reverse from lining fabric

B ----- A

thumb
gusset

slash

MITTEN BACK
(add ¼-inch seam allowance)
cut one from mitten fabric
cut one from lining fabric

cut one reverse from mitten fabric
cut one reverse from lining fabric

B — — — — A

MITTEN THUMB
(add ¼-inch seam allowance)
cut one from mitten fabric
cut one from lining fabric

cut one reverse from mitten fabric
cut one reverse from lining fabric

MITTEN PATTERNS

1 SQUARE = 1 INCH

Gingerbread Jar

WHAT YOU NEED

Glass jar with lid; newspapers; tracing paper
Pencil; scissors; tape; disposable foam plate
Acrylic glass paints in green, white, red, brown, and
    black; paintbrush

HERE'S HOW

1 Wash and dry the glassware. Avoid touching the areas to
be painted.

2 Cover the work surface with newspapers. Trace the
pattern, *below right*, onto tracing paper. (If necessary,
reduce or enlarge the pattern on a copy machine to fit the
jar.) Trim any extra paper from the design. Tape the
pattern to the inside of the jar.

3 On a foam plate, mix a small amount of green with white
to make light green. Paint the background going around
the gingerbread man shape. While the paint is wet, add a
few swirls of white paint. Paint the lid light mint green.
Highlight with white. Let dry.

4 Paint the gingerbread man brown. Let the paint dry.
Paint in the details of the gingerbread
man, the background, and the lid.
To mix pink tones, stir a dab of
red into white without mixing
completely. Dip the handle end
of a paintbrush into the paint
and dot on the surface. Let the
paint dry.

This wintry jar is perfect for the season's sweet surprises. Adaptable to any shape container, this gingerbread character can dance on the jar of your choice.

GINGERBREAD MAN
JAR PATTERN

Crocheted Heart Jackets

NOTES: *Directions are for child size 2; changes for size 4 and size 6 follow in parentheses. Finished chest size = 28(30, 32) inches. Finished length = 16½(18½, 20½) inches. The single-crochet jacket is worked in one piece to the underarm. Embroider hearts after the crocheting is complete. Skill Level: Beginner.*

WHAT YOU NEED

Patons Astra 100% acrylic yarn (50-gm./163-m. skein): 4(5, 6) skeins of red (2762) and 4(5, 6) skeins of white (2751)
Size 5/F (3.75 mm) aluminum crochet hook or size needed to obtain gauge
Tapestry needle
Five ½-inch heart buttons

GAUGE: **In sc, 18 sts = 4 inches; 19 rows = 4 inches.**

HERE'S HOW

1 JACKET: Beginning at lower edge with red, ch 127(136, 145). Sc in second ch from hook and in each ch across = 126(135, 144) sts; turn. **Row 2 (WS):** Ch 1, sc in each sc across; turn. Rep Row 2 for 32(36, 42) more rows. Fasten off red. With the RS facing, join white with sl st in first sc. Ch 1, sc in each sc across; turn. Work 3 more white sc rows; fasten off. Work 4 red sc rows. Change to white for remainder of jacket body. Work even to 9(10½, 12) inches from beg.

2 RIGHT FRONT: Ch 1, sc in each of first 32(34, 36) sts; turn. Work even to 13½(15½, 17½) inches from beg, ending with a RS row. **For Neck Shaping:** Ch 1, sc in each of first 24(26, 28) sts; sc2tog; leave rem 6 sts unworked = 25(27, 29) sts; turn. Cont est pat, dec 1 st at neck edge EOR 5 times. Work even on rem 20(22, 24) sts until piece measures 16(18, 20) inches from beg. Fasten off.

Your little sweetheart will look like a doll (hers!) with these matching crocheted sweaters.

CROCHET ABBREVIATIONS
Dc = double crochet
Hdc = half double crochet
Rep = repeat
Sc = single crochet
Tre = triple crochet

Crocheted Heart Jackets instructions are continued on pages 84–87.

Bundle-Up Set

WHAT YOU NEED

Tracing paper; pencil; scissors
Felt in bright pink, bright green, and periwinkle
Yellow embroidery floss; embroidery needle
Purchased knit hat and mittens
Two ¼-inch-diameter periwinkle buttons

HERE'S HOW

1 Trace leaf and flower patterns, *below*, separately onto tracing paper; cut out. Use patterns to cut pieces from felt: From pink, cut three circles for hat flower center and mitten flowers; from green, cut two large leaves and two small leaves; from periwinkle, cut one hat flower.

2 Use six strands of floss for all embroidery stitches and to attach buttons. Center one pink circle on the periwinkle flower. Attach circle to flower with approximately 14 French knots, sewing through both felt layers and wrapping floss around needle twice for each knot. Make seven French knots around the edge of each remaining mitten flower circle.

3 Arrange periwinkle flower and two large leaves on the hat, referring to photograph for placement. With yellow embroidery floss, secure the felt pieces to the hat with long straight stitches centered on the leaves and flower petals.

4 Position one bright pink circle and one small leaf on each mitten. Sew the leaves to the mittens with long straight stitches centered on the leaves. Sew a button through the center of each pink circle.

Send little ones out to play in this colorful hat and mittens. The store-bought set is brightened with felt flowers and embroidery.

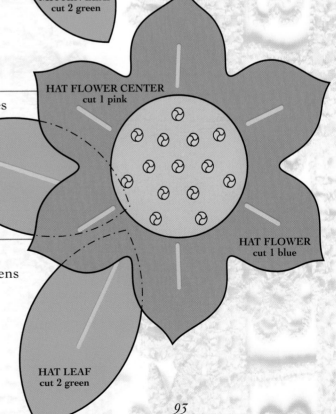

MITTEN FLOWER
cut 2 pink

MITTEN LEAF
cut 2 green

HAT FLOWER CENTER
cut 1 pink

HAT FLOWER
cut 1 blue

HAT LEAF
cut 2 green

93

Package Pillows

Turn any sofa or chair into a holiday retreat with these fun gift-package pillows.

What You Need

2/3 yard of muslin
Measuring tape
Scissors
Thread
Pins
Fiberfill or purchased 11-inch square pillow form
  (available at some fabric stores)
2/3 yard of plum-color velvet
Sheer ribbon
Purchased fabric ornaments, optional

Here's How

1 **To make the large pillow,** cut muslin into six 12-inch squares.

2 Right sides together and using ½-inch seam allowances, sew four squares together in a row. Sew ends together to form a continuous loop.

3 Right sides together, pin another 12-inch square to top, matching corners to seams. Stitch.

4 Right sides together, pin remaining square to bottom, matching corners to seams. Stitch, leaving a 5-inch opening. Turn right side out. Stuff with fiberfill; whipstitch the opening closed.

5 For pillow, cut velvet into six 12-inch squares.

6 Sew velvet pillow as for muslin form, leaving an 8-inch opening in top piece. Turn right side out. Insert pillow form in opening; whipstitch closed.

7 Tie sheer ribbon around pillow. Hand-tack purchased fabric ornaments to pillow top, if desired.

8 **To make the small pillow,** use 6-inch squares instead of 12-inch squares. To create the checkerboard, combine four 3½-inch squares of coordinating fabrics for each side. Sew together using ½-inch seam allowances. Finish as for the large pillow.

Candy-Filled Gifts

WHAT YOU NEED

Pencil
Open-style cookie cutters
Lightweight cardboard
Scissors
Transparent tape
Nuts or small candies
Corsage bag (available at floral shops)
8 inches of ribbon

HERE'S HOW

1 Draw around a cookie cutter onto lightweight cardboard. Cut out the shape. Tape the cardboard to the back of the cookie cutter. Fill the cookie cutter with nuts or candies. With cutter lying flat, slide the corsage bag around the cookie cutter and tie a ribbon bow around the open end of the bag.

Cookie cutters filled with favorite goodies are easy-to-make gifts.

Holiday Kitchen Trims

Warm a snowy evening by creating this winter centerpiece.

WHAT YOU NEED

Grater, sieve, or other kitchen tool
Artificial or real holly or other winter greenery
Hot-glue gun; hot-glue sticks
Candle (optional)

HERE'S HOW

1 Wash the kitchen tool and let it dry. Arrange the greenery and glue only the greenery together. Glue the arranged piece to the kitchen tool. Place a candle inside if desired.

Painted Bottles

What You Need

Glass bottle with embossed pattern
Surface conditioner and cleaner, such as Perm-Enamel
Retarder, such as Perm-Enamel
**Enamel paints, such as Delta Ceramdecor Air-Dry
    Perm-Enamels, in hunter green, true green, eggplant,
    light burgundy, and 14K gold**
Satin and gloss glaze, such as Perm-Enamel
Small paintbrushes

Here's How

1 Wash bottle with warm soapy water and dry thoroughly. Clean outer surface with surface conditioner and cleaner; let dry.

2 Use paint directly from the jar or, if a more transparent paint is desired, mix paint with satin glaze. Do not add water. Add a few drops of retarder to paints to extend the drying time to approximately 10–20 minutes; however, too much retarder will thin the paint too much. Brush satin glaze over the areas to paint; let dry. Paint over the satin glaze, covering all areas with one color before moving on to the next color. Add highlights with 14K gold; let dry. Seal painted areas with gloss glaze; let dry 1 hour, then apply another coat. It is safe to fill the bottle immediately, but wait a week before washing it. After a week it will be safe to wash in the top rack of the dishwasher.

When glass bottles have embossed patterns, decorating them is paint-by-number easy.

Hot and Spicy Nuts

Hot and Spicy Nuts are a great gift and easy to prepare. For a fun presentation, glue a personalized label on the jar and use raffia to tie a pair of colorful peppers around the rim.

WHAT YOU NEED

- 1 teaspoon ground coriander
- 1 teaspoon ground cumin
- 1/2 teaspoon salt
- 1/4 teaspoon pepper
- 1/8 teaspoon ground red pepper (cayenne)
- 2 cups raw peanuts (or raw cashews, almonds, or macadamia nuts)
- 1 tablespoon cooking oil

HERE'S HOW

1 Preheat oven to 300°F. Stir together coriander, cumin, salt, pepper, and red pepper in a small bowl; set aside. Place nuts in a 13×9×2-inch baking pan. Drizzle with oil, stirring to coat. Sprinkle with spice mixture; toss lightly.

2 Bake in preheated oven about 20 minutes or until lightly toasted, stirring once or twice. Cool in pan for 15 minutes. Turn out onto paper towels; cool completely. Store, covered, in a cool place. Makes 2 cups.

wishing you a HOT & SPICY holiday

from the kitchen of
HEATHER

Papaya-Rum Chutney

WHAT YOU NEED

    5 or 6 papayas
    4 large cloves garlic, quartered
    4 large jalapeño peppers, peeled, seeded, and chopped*
    2 cups packed light brown sugar
1 1/2 cups cider vinegar
  1/2 cup light rum

HERE'S HOW

1 Halve papayas; scoop out seeds. Peel papayas. Chop and
   measure 6 cups. Place in a 4- to 6-quart Dutch oven or
   kettle. Add garlic. Add about 1/2 cup peppers to kettle.
   (*Jalapeño peppers contain volatile oils that can burn your
   skin and eyes. Avoid direct contact with them by wearing
   plastic gloves and wash hands with soap after handling.)
   Add brown sugar and vinegar.

2 Heat mixture over medium heat to boiling. Reduce heat;
   add rum. Boil gently, uncovered, for 30 to 40 minutes
   or until desired consistency. Ladle chutney into hot,
   clean half-pint canning jars, leaving 1/2-inch headspace.
   Wipe rims; adjust lids. Process in a boiling-water canner
   for 10 minutes (start timing when water begins to boil).
   Remove jars from the canner; cool on wire racks.
   Makes 5 half-pints (70 one-tablespoon servings).

A great gift for grilling enthusiasts, this chutney adds a wonderfully spicy flavor to meats. Place a jar of the condiment in a metal container that will allow for easy transport. Tie on a wooden spoon with raffia and tuck in a few fresh chile peppers.

Cherry-Hazelnut Snowballs

All decked out in sparkly cellophane and beaded wire, Cherry-Hazelnut Snowballs are a sweet indulgence for the holidays. The rich spread of cream cheese and butter rolled in coconut tastes terrific on shortbread cookies. To make the snowflake trims, cut small pieces of beaded wire and glue them together.

WHAT YOU NEED

1   8-ounce package cream cheese, softened
1/2 cup butter (no substitutes), softened
1/4 cup sifted powdered sugar
1   tablespoon milk
1/3 cup snipped dried cherries and/or finely chopped dried figs
1/3 cup toasted hazelnuts (filberts) or almonds, chopped
3/4 cup coconut
64 shortbread cookies

HERE'S HOW

1   Combine cream cheese, butter, powdered sugar, and milk in a medium mixing bowl. Beat with an electric mixer on medium speed about 1 minute or until combined. Stir in cherries and/or figs and hazelnuts.

2   Shape mixture into two equal-size balls, 3 inches in diameter. Refrigerate the blended mixture for 20 to 30 minutes. Roll balls in coconut. Cover and store in the refrigerator for up to 3 days. Serve with shortbread cookies. Makes 2 balls (32 cookies each).

Gingerbread Cookie Mix

WHAT YOU NEED

- 5 cups all-purpose flour
- 1 cup sugar
- 2 teaspoons baking powder
- 2 teaspoons ground ginger
- 1 teaspoon baking soda
- 1 teaspoon ground cinnamon
- 1 teaspoon ground cloves
- 1 quart plastic bag
- Decorative candies; cellophane packets
- Scissors or crafts knife
- 1 12½-inch square of plain paper
- 1 12½-inch square of corrugated art paper
- Paper punch; pencil; thick white crafts glue
- 3 yards of red metallic cording
- Small cookie cutter

Your holiday gift will be twice as nice when you present this Gingerbread Cookie Mix in a pyramid-shape box of white corrugated cardboard laced with red metallic cording.

HERE'S HOW

1 For the mix, combine flour, sugar, baking powder, ginger, baking soda, cinnamon, and cloves in a large mixing bowl. Store in an airtight container for up to 6 months at room temperature.

2 Transfer half of the mixture to a 1-quart plastic bag. Seal the bag. Wrap assorted decorative candies in separate cellophane packets.

3 **To make a box**, see the pattern and diagram on *page 107*. Fold the 12½-inch square of plain paper on dashed lines. Unfold.

Gingerbread Cookie Mix instructions are continued on pages 106–107.

3-D Stand-ups

For a three-dimensional effect, pair snowflakes or trees to make stand-up ornaments. Fold the trees flat to fit in a transparent envelope to spread a little joy.

Tracing paper; pencil; scissors
Assorted art and construction papers
4¾×6½-inch transparent envelopes (available in stationery and art stores)
Thick white crafts glue

HERE'S HOW

1 Trace full-size patterns, *below*, onto tracing paper; cut out. Trace around patterns onto paper, tracing two shapes for each snowflake and tree stand-up. Cut out shapes slightly inside traced lines. Cut a slit in each snowflake marked on pattern. Cut a slit on one tree piece from trunk to dot and on one tree from top to dot.

2 Slide snowflake and tree pieces together. Spread pieces to stand. To mail, flatten stand-up pieces to insert in envelope. For gift wrap trim, glue a shape to each side of a wrapped box.

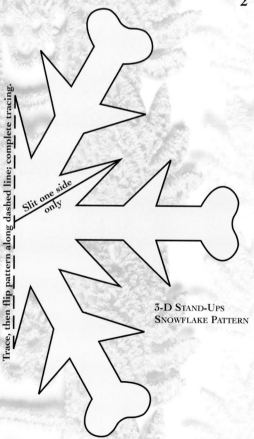

Slit one side only

Trace, then flip pattern along dashed line; complete tracing.

3-D STAND-UPS
SNOWFLAKE PATTERN

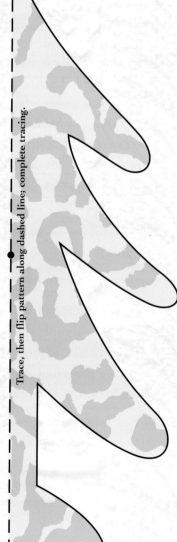

3-D STAND-UPS
TREE PATTERN

Trace, then flip pattern along dashed line; complete tracing.

Wondrous Wraps

When plain wrapping paper isn't special enough, try one of these clever gift wraps. Top boxes with sprigs of evergreen and holly for natural elegance. Metallic pipe cleaners sparkle as bows and accents on simply shaped tags. Put buttons to good use by fastening ribbon-tied gifts and transform scraps of paper or felt into miniature packages—all perfect for extra-wow gift tags and greeting cards.

Natural Beauties

WHAT YOU NEED

Box with lid
Paint and paintbrush or art paper in desired colors
Scissors; glue stick (for paper-covered box)
Floral wire; greenery
Ribbon or tape

HERE'S HOW

1 For painted box, paint box and lid and let dry. For paper-covered box, cut pieces of art paper to fit each side of box, allowing extra paper to overlap pieces slightly. Glue in place.

2 Wire together greens. Tie to the box using ribbon or tape the topper in place.

Button It Up

WHAT YOU NEED

Solid-color paper
Narrow ribbon
Scissors
Large buttons with large holes
Awl

HERE'S HOW

1 Wrap gifts with a solid-color paper. For the red package, thread narrow ribbon through a button, then finish with a big bow. For the green package, poke holes in box lid and base to correspond with chosen buttons. Use ribbon to attach a button to each set of holes. Close box by wrapping a ribbon around buttons; tie into bow.

Wondrous Wraps instructions are continued on pages 112–113.

NATURAL
BEAUTIES

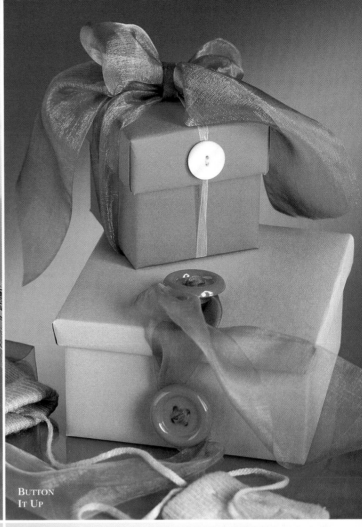

BUTTON
IT UP

PUTTIN' ON
THE GLITZ

TIE-IT-UP
GIFT CARDS

Wondrous Wraps

Silvery pipe cleaners that resemble old-fashioned tinsel add sparkle to gift containers. Use pipe cleaners as trim, or make bows for toppers.

Puttin' on the Glitz
Pipe Cleaner Bows

WHAT YOU NEED FOR ONE BOW

9 decorative pipe cleaners
Thick white crafts glue

HERE'S HOW

1 Lay eight pipe cleaners side by side in a bundle, aligning ends. Fasten bundle together by twisting a ninth pipe cleaner around bundle center. Position ends of ninth pipe cleaner to extend perpendicularly. Bend half of the pipe cleaners to form curved loops with ends overlapping the center.

2 Wrap one-half of ninth pipe cleaner around ends of eight loops several times, securing them to center and leaving a short tail. Repeat with remaining pipe cleaners, securing with remaining half of ninth pipe cleaner. Twist tails of ninth pipe cleaner together. Shape loops; glue bow to box top. Glue pipe cleaners to box edges as desired.

Puttin' on the Glitz
Ornament Tags

WHAT YOU NEED

Art paper; scissors
Pipe cleaners
Thick white crafts glue
Paper punch

HERE'S HOW

1 Cut simple ornament-shape tags from art paper. Bend pipe cleaner trims to decorate, and glue to tags.

2 Punch a hole in the tag. Use a pipe cleaner to attach each tag to a package.

Tie-It-Up Gift Cards

WHAT YOU NEED

Art paper
Polyester stuffing or potpourri
Small piece of felt
Needle
Thread
Awl
Silver cording

HERE'S HOW

1 Fold art paper to the desired card size (the cards, *right*, are 5×5 and 4×9 inches), using a second color slightly smaller if desired.

2 Cut two pieces of felt, approximately 2½×2½ inches for a square package or 1¾×3½ inches for a rectangular package.

3 Using a running stitch, and with wrong sides together, sew three sides of the felt together. Stuff with a small amount of batting. Sew the remaining side closed.

4 Poke small holes in the card front at sides of gift. Lace silver cording through the holes, over gift, and tie in a bow. The potpourri-filled gifts double as sachets.

Large or small, any size card is festive when trimmed with a gift. Fill mini packages with potpourri to double as sachets.

Polka-Dot Box

Rather than wrap gifts with run-of-the-mill holiday paper, surprise friends and family with personal touches. Cover a gift box with two colors of cellophane and tie it with a sheer bow.

WHAT YOU NEED

Papier-mâché box
White paint
Paintbrush
2 sheets blue cellophane
Small lid or round cookie cutter
Permanent black marker
Cutting board
Crafts knife or circle-cutout compass
2 sheets green cellophane
Sheer ribbon

HERE'S HOW

1 Paint papier-mâché box white; let dry.

2 Lay a sheet of blue cellophane on a cutting board; mark circles randomly on the cellophane by drawing around a small lid or cookie cutter. Cut out the circles using a crafts knife or use a circle-cutout compass.

3 Place a sheet of green cellophane over the blue. Wrap the box base with the two layers, with the blue sheet on the outside. Repeat for the box top, reversing the colors (make circle cutouts in green cellophane and wrap the box top with green sheet on outside).

4 Tie with a sheer ribbon.

Transform a brown paper sack into a fun gift bag with ho-ho-ho flair.

Jolly Gift Bags

WHAT YOU NEED

Tracing paper; pencil
Scraps of fabric in red and white
Paper-backed fusible webbing; scissors; brown lunch bag
Tube-style paints in shiny white, shiny black,
   and crystal

HERE'S HOW

1 Trace pattern, *page 116,* separately on tracing paper (broken lines indicate overlap). Mark right side of each pattern. Turn pattern right side down on paper side of fusible web; trace around patterns.

2 Cut out pieces ¼ inch outside of traced lines and fuse to wrong side of fabric. Cut out on traced lines; peel off paper. Position pieces on bag and fuse in place.

3 Draw squiggly eyebrows with shiny white paint, make dot eyes with shiny black paint, and outline hat and beard with crystal paint "stitch" lines.

JOLLY GIFT BAGS
PATTERN

Use a computer scanner or copy center to create unique, memory-evoking photo wrapping paper.

Picture Perfect

WHAT YOU NEED

Photographs to photocopy
White paper
Tape

HERE'S HOW

1 On a photocopier, duplicate a photo or enlarge holiday expressions to fill one sheet of paper. From the photocopied sheet, make multiple copies to wrap the package. Tape the copies together to wrap a gift.

Decorative Die-Cut Cards

WHAT YOU NEED

Tracing paper; pencil; crafts knife; cutting mat
White card with envelope; small paper punch
Christmas cards; scissors; tape
Heavy white paper; glue stick

HERE'S HOW

1 Trace a pattern, *below*, onto tracing paper. Lay the tracing paper on a cutting mat and cut shapes from background using a crafts knife, leaving background intact.

2 Lay pattern over the front of the card and trace inside the pattern. Open the card, lay it on the cutting mat, and cut the shapes from the background. Make the dots in the center of the poinsettia with a small paper punch, placing the design where the paper punch will reach the flower center.

3 With the pattern, trace shapes onto patterned portions of Christmas cards. Cut out small shapes ⅛ inch beyond traced line. Cut the flower center and the petals each from one piece.

4 Tape the card pieces behind the cutout shapes. Cut a piece of paper slightly smaller than the card front. Glue paper piece over the taped card pieces. Let the glue dry.

Recycle last year's Christmas cards using these patterns to fill the tree and poinsettia cutouts.

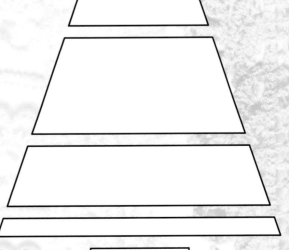

POINSETTIA PATTERN   TREE PATTERN

To: Tim
From: Amy

To: Holly
From: Betsy

To: Scott
From: SANTA

Scalloped Paper Tags

WHAT YOU NEED

Straight and decorative-edge scissors
Paper in red, green, white, and ivory
Small round paper punch
Paper punches
Thick white crafts glue

HERE'S HOW

1 Using straight or decorative-edge scissors, cut shapes from ivory or white paper.

2 Using the photograph for inspiration, cut additional shapes from colored papers. To hold paper layers together, punch two holes through the layers and weave a paper strip through the holes.

3 To make lacy edges, cut with a scalloped-edge scissors. Use a small paper punch to punch holes within the scallops as shown, *below*.

4 Decorate the tags by gluing with punched paper shapes.

Snippets of paper trimmed with paper-punched lace edges make keepsake gift tags.

Holiday Breads & Hearty Soups

❦

"Christmas is not a
time nor a season, but a
state of mind. To cherish
peace and goodwill, to be
plenteous in mercy, is to
have the real spirit
of Christmas."

—Calvin Coolidge

❦

Cream Cheese Braids

The perfect addition to Christmas brunch, this breakfast braid is filled with pineapple and topped with vanilla glaze. As a substitute for the pineapple, use chopped canned pears.

WHAT YOU NEED

- 4 cups all-purpose flour
- 2 packages active dry yeast
- 1 8-ounce carton dairy sour cream
- ¹/₂ cup water
- ¹/₂ cup butter
- ¹/₂ cup sugar
- 1 teaspoon salt
- 2 eggs
- 1 8-ounce package cream cheese, softened
- ¹/₃ cup sugar
- 1 egg yolk
- 1 teaspoon vanilla
- 1 8-ounce can crushed pineapple, well drained
  Vanilla Glaze
- ¹/₄ cup sliced almonds

HERE'S HOW

1 In a large bowl, combine 2 cups of the flour and the yeast; set aside. In a medium saucepan, combine sour cream, water, butter, the ¹/₂ cup sugar, and salt over medium-low heat just until warm (120°F to 130°F). Add warm mixture to flour mixture along with the 2 eggs; stir until well combined. Stir in remaining flour. Cover tightly; chill overnight.

2 For filling, in a medium bowl beat cream cheese, the ¹/₃ cup sugar, egg yolk, and vanilla. Stir in pineapple; set aside.

3 Preheat oven to 375°F. Divide dough into three portions. On a well-floured surface, roll one dough portion to a 12×9-inch rectangle (keep remaining dough chilled until ready to use). Grease two large baking sheets; set aside.

4 Spread a scant ²/₃ cup cream cheese mixture on rolled dough to within ¹/₂ inch of edges. Roll up, starting with a long side. Seal seam; place, seam side down, on prepared baking sheet. Cut slits 2 inches apart and halfway through loaf. Repeat with remaining dough and filling. Cover; let rise in warm place until nearly doubled (45 to 60 minutes). Bake in a 375°F oven for about 20 minutes or until golden.

Cool on wire racks. While warm, drizzle with Vanilla Glaze; sprinkle with almonds. Makes 3 loaves (36 servings).

5 VANILLA GLAZE: In medium bowl, combine 1½ cups sifted powdered sugar, 1 tablespoon milk, and 1 teaspoon vanilla. Stir in additional milk, 1 teaspoon at a time, until of drizzling consistency.

6 TO MAKE AHEAD: Prepare and bake as directed; cool completely. Do not glaze or sprinkle with almonds. Wrap in foil. Place in freezer bags. Seal, label, and freeze for up to 3 months. To serve, place on baking sheet; bake in a 375°F oven for 15 to 20 minutes or until heated through. Drizzle with glaze; sprinkle with nuts.

Orange Cherry Twists

Sweet cherries and tangy orange juice combine for just the right flavor to make these twists a family favorite—any time of the year.

WHAT YOU NEED

4 to 4 1/2 cups all-purpose flour
2 packages active dry yeast
1/2 cup milk
1/3 cup sugar
1/3 cup butter or margarine
1/2 teaspoon salt
2 eggs
1/2 cup orange juice
3/4 cup dried tart red cherries or cranberries, chopped
2/3 cup sugar
1/4 cup butter or margarine, softened
1 tablespoon all-purpose flour
1 tablespoon finely shredded orange peel (set aside)
Orange Icing

HERE'S HOW

1 Combine 2 cups of the flour and the yeast in a large mixing bowl; set aside.

2 Heat and stir milk, the 1/3 cup sugar, the 1/3 cup butter or margarine, and salt in a medium saucepan until warm (120°F to 130°F) and butter or margarine almost melts. Add to flour mixture. Add eggs and orange juice. Beat with an electric mixer on low to medium speed for 30 seconds, scraping the sides of the bowl. Beat on high speed for 3 minutes. Using a wooden spoon, stir in dried cherries or cranberries and as much of the remaining flour as you can.

3 Turn dough out onto a lightly floured surface. Knead in enough of the remaining flour to make a moderately stiff dough that is smooth and elastic (6 to 8 minutes total). Shape dough into a ball. Place dough in a lightly greased bowl, turning once to grease entire surface. Cover and let rise in a warm place about 1 hour until doubled.

4 Punch dough down; turn out onto a lightly floured surface. Divide dough in half. Cover and let rest for 10 minutes. If baking immediately, grease two foil-lined baking sheets; set aside.

5 For filling, combine the ⅔ cup sugar, the ¼ cup butter or margarine, the 1 tablespoon flour, and orange peel. Roll each half of dough into a 14×10-inch rectangle. Spread filling lengthwise over half of each rectangle. Fold dough in half lengthwise, covering the filling. Cut each rectangle into fourteen 1-inch-wide strips. Holding a strip at both ends, carefully twist the top in one direction and the bottom in the opposite direction. Repeat for remaining strips.

6 If baking immediately, place strips on prepared baking sheets, pressing ends down. Cover and let rise in a warm place about 30 minutes until nearly doubled. Bake in a 375°F oven for 15 to 18 minutes or until lightly browned.

7 To make ahead, cover twists with oiled waxed paper, then with plastic wrap; chill for 2 to 24 hours. Uncover twists and let stand at room temperature 30 minutes. Break bubbles with a greased wooden toothpick before baking.

8 Remove twists from baking sheets and place on a wire rack. If serving immediately, drizzle with Orange Icing. Or place cooled twists in a freezer container or bag and freeze for up to 1 month. To reheat, place twists on two baking sheets. Bake in a 350°F oven for about 10 minutes or until heated through. Drizzle with Orange Icing. Makes 28.

9 ORANGE ICING: Stir together 1 cup sifted powdered sugar, 1 teaspoon finely shredded orange peel, and enough orange juice (2 to 3 tablespoons) to make the icing of drizzling consistency.

Lemon Bread

Dainty sugar-glazed slices of bread make a spectacular breakfast treat. To give this bread as a gift, place a bag of the dry ingredients in foil baking pans, top with fresh lemons, and include instructions for preparation. Tie with a ribbon for a well received holiday treat.

WHAT YOU NEED

3½ cups all-purpose flour
1½ cups granulated sugar
 4 teaspoons poppy seeds
 1 tablespoon baking powder
 1 teaspoon salt
 1 teaspoon baking soda
½ teaspoon ground nutmeg
 1 lemon
 1 egg
¾ cup milk
¼ cup cooking oil
½ cup sifted powdered sugar

HERE'S HOW

1 Preheat oven to 350°F. Combine flour, granulated sugar, poppy seeds, baking powder, salt, soda, and nutmeg in a large bowl. Make a well in center of dry mixture; set aside.

2 Finely shred lemon peel to yield 1½ teaspoons peel. Squeeze lemon to yield 7 teaspoons lemon juice.

3 Combine egg, milk, cooking oil, 1 teaspoon of the finely shredded lemon peel and 1 tablespoon of the lemon juice in another bowl. Add egg mixture all at once to the dry mixture. Sir just until moistened (batter should be lumpy).

4 Grease bottom and ½ inch up the sides of four 5¾×3×2-inch loaf pans or two 8×4×2-inch loaf pans. Spoon batter into pans. Bake in the preheated oven for 30 to 35 minutes for 5¾×3×2-inch pans or 45 to 50 minutes for the 8×4×2-inch pan or until a wooden toothpick inserted near the center comes out clean. Cool in pans on a wire rack for 10 minutes. Remove from pans. Cool completely on wire rack. Wrap and store overnight.

5 Before serving, combine sifted powdered sugar, the remaining ½ teaspoon of the finely shredded lemon peel, and enough remaining lemon juice (2 to 3 teaspoons) to make icing of drizzling consistency. Drizzle over the loaf or loaves. Garnish with lemon peel strips, if desired. Makes 4 small loaves or 2 large loaves (32 servings).

Drizzled Delights

These savory whole wheat buns are perfect mates to a bowl of your favorite hot and hearty soup or chili.

Sweet Onion Wheat Buns

WHAT YOU NEED

2	tablespoons butter or margarine
2	teaspoons brown sugar
1	large onion, thinly sliced
1	cup all-purpose flour
3/4	cup whole wheat flour
1 1/2	teaspoons baking powder
3/4	teaspoon salt
3/4	teaspoon dried sage, crushed
1/2	teaspoon baking soda
1	beaten egg
1	8-ounce carton plain low-fat yogurt
2	tablespoons brown sugar

HERE'S HOW

1 In a large skillet combine butter and the 2 teaspoons brown sugar. Cook and stir over medium heat about 1 minute or just until blended. Add the onion. Cook, uncovered, over low heat for 10 to 12 minutes or until onion is very tender and light brown, stirring occasionally. Set aside some of the smaller onion rings for garnish. Don't drain off the margarine. Chop the remaining onion.

2 In a large bowl combine all-purpose flour, whole wheat flour, baking powder, salt, sage, and baking soda. In a small bowl combine the egg, yogurt, and the 2 tablespoons brown sugar. Add the egg mixture to the flour mixture; stir just until moistened. Stir in chopped onion and margarine mixture. (The dough will be slightly sticky.)

3 Preheat oven to 400°F. With a 1/4- or 1/3-cup measure, scoop dough into mounds onto a greased baking sheet. With wet hands, form mounds into rounded buns, about 1 inch thick. Top with the reserved onion rings, pressing them gently into buns.

4 Bake in preheated oven about 12 minutes or until the buns are golden brown and a wooden toothpick inserted in the center comes out clean. Serve warm. Makes 8 to 10 buns.

Ginger-Date Pumpkin Loaves

 2 cups all-purpose flour
 1 cup sugar
 1 tablespoon finely chopped
     crystallized ginger
2½ teaspoons baking powder
 ½ teaspoon baking soda
 ½ teaspoon ground nutmeg
 ¼ teaspoon salt
 1 cup canned pumpkin
 ½ cup milk
 2 eggs
 ⅓ cup shortening
 1 cup chopped pitted dates
     Spiced Glaze

HERE'S HOW

1 Preheat oven to 350°F. In a medium mixing bowl combine
  1 cup of the flour, sugar, ginger, baking powder, baking
  soda, nutmeg, and salt. Add pumpkin, milk, eggs, and
  shortening. Beat with an electric mixer on low to medium
  speed for 30 seconds. Beat on high speed for 2 minutes,
  scraping bowl occasionally. Add the remaining flour; beat
  until well mixed. Stir in the dates.

2 Pour the batter into five 4½×2½×1½-inch loaf pans or two
  8×4×2-inch loaf pans. Bake in preheated oven for 35 to
  40 minutes for smaller loaves or 45 minutes for larger loaves
  or until a wooden toothpick inserted near centers comes
  out clean. Cool in pans on wire racks for 10 minutes.
  Remove from pans and cool completely. Wrap bread and
  store overnight at room temperature. Before serving, drizzle
  with Spiced Glaze. Makes 5 small loaves or 2 large loaves.

3 SPICED GLAZE: In a small mixing bowl stir together ½ cup
  sifted powdered sugar and ⅛ teaspoon ground ginger. Stir
  in enough water (2 to 3 teaspoons) to make icing of
  drizzling consistency.

Vanocka Braid

This layered braided bread, with its name derived from the Czech word for Christmas, is sprinkled with sliced almonds.

WHAT YOU NEED

5¹/₂	to 6 cups all-purpose flour
1	package active dry yeast
1¹/₄	cups milk
²/₃	cup sugar
¹/₄	cup margarine or butter
¹/₂	teaspoon salt
2	eggs
1	egg white
¹/₄	teaspoon ground mace
1¹/₂	cups light raisins
1	teaspoon finely shredded lemon peel
1	beaten egg yolk
¹/₄	cup sliced almonds

HERE'S HOW

1 In a large bowl combine 2½ cups of the flour and the yeast; set aside. In a saucepan heat and stir the milk, sugar, margarine, and salt just until warm and margarine almost melts. Add to flour mixture. Add the 2 eggs, the egg white, and mace. Beat with an electric mixer on low to medium speed for 30 seconds, scraping bowl. Beat on high speed for 3 minutes. Using a spoon, stir in raisins, lemon peel, and as much remaining flour as you can.

2 On a floured surface, knead in enough of the remaining flour to make a moderately stiff dough that is smooth and elastic (6 to 8 minutes total). Shape into a ball. Place in a greased bowl; turn once. Cover and let rise in a warm place until doubled (1 to 1½ hours).

3 Punch dough down. Turn the dough out onto a lightly floured surface. Divide in half. Cover and let rest 10 minutes. Grease 2 large baking sheets. Set half of the dough aside.

4 Divide the remaining half of dough in half. Cut one of the portions into thirds. Roll each third into an evenly thick 18-inch rope. To braid, line up the 3 ropes, 1 inch apart, on a prepared baking sheet. Starting in the middle, loosely bring left rope underneath center rope; lay it down. Bring the right rope under the new center rope; lay it down.

Repeat to center. On the opposite end, braid by bringing the outside ropes alternately over center rope to the center. Press ends together to seal and tuck under. Stretch braid to a length of 11 inches. Divide the other portion of dough into quarters. Roll three of the four pieces into evenly thick 14-inch ropes. Braid loosely; press ends together to seal and tuck under. Stretch braid to a length of 9 inches. Brush top of first braid with enough water to moisten; place second braid on top of first braid. Cut remaining quarter of dough into thirds. Roll each third into an evenly thick 12-inch rope. Braid loosely; press the ends together to seal and tuck under. Stretch braid to a length of 7 inches. Brush top of second braid with enough water to moisten; place third braid on top of second braid.

5 Repeat shaping directions with the other half of the dough. Cover braids and let them rise until nearly double (30 to 45 minutes).

6 Preheat oven to 350°F. Brush braids with a mixture of beaten egg yolk and 2 teaspoons water. Sprinkle with sliced almonds. Bake for 15 minutes. Cover loosely with foil. Bake 20 to 25 minutes more or until the bread tests done. Cool on wire rack. Serve warm or cool. Makes 2 loaves.

Blueberry-Orange Bread

Fresh berries deliciously flavor and color this good-morning bread. Serve it with holiday brunch fare or at Christmas tea.

WHAT YOU NEED

- 2 cups all-purpose flour
- 1 teaspoon baking powder
- 1/2 teaspoon salt
- 1/4 teaspoon baking soda
- 2 tablespoons butter, cut up
- 1/4 cup boiling water
- 1 egg, slightly beaten
- 1 cup sugar
- 1/2 cup orange juice
- 1 cup fresh blueberries

HERE'S HOW

1 Grease the bottom and 1/2 inch up the sides of an 8×4×2-inch loaf pan; set aside.

2 Preheat oven to 350°F. In a large bowl, stir together flour, baking powder, salt, and baking soda; make a well in center and set aside. Stir together butter and boiling water until butter is melted. In a medium bowl, combine egg, sugar, and orange juice; stir in butter mixture. Add to the dry ingredients, stirring just until moistened. Fold in blueberries. Spoon the batter into the prepared pan.

3 Bake in preheated oven about 60 minutes or until a toothpick inserted near the center comes out clean. Cool 10 minutes. Remove loaf from pan. Cool completely on a wire rack. Wrap in foil and store overnight. Makes 1 loaf (16 slices).

TEST KITCHEN TIP: Frozen blueberries work in this recipe, too, but they may "bleed" when you fold them into the batter.

Oyster Stew

WHAT YOU NEED

- 1/2 cup sliced leek or chopped onion
- 1 medium potato, diced
- 1 cup water
- 1/2 teaspoon instant chicken bouillon granules
- 1/4 teaspoon white pepper
- 2 12-ounce cans evaporated fat-free milk
- 1 pint shucked oysters
- 1 tablespoon snipped fresh parsley
- 2 teaspoons butter-flavor sprinkles (optional)

HERE'S HOW

1 In a 3-quart saucepan, combine leek, potato, water, bouillon granules, and white pepper. Bring mixture to boiling; reduce heat. Cover and simmer about 7 minutes or until potatoes are tender. Do not drain.

2 Stir in evaporated milk; cook over medium heat for 5 minutes. Add the undrained oysters. Cook about 5 minutes more or until the edges of the oysters curl, stirring frequently. Stir in parsley and, if desired, butter-flavor sprinkles. Serve immediately in soup bowls. Makes 6 servings.

Unlike traditional stew that calls for heavy cream, this tasty version uses evaporated fat-free milk — slashing calories and fat grams but leaving the rich flavor of this holiday favorite.

Tomato-Basil Soup

This cold-weather soup is inspired by the cuisine of Northern Italy, where tomatoes and basil are popular ingredients. Also try it during summer months when you can use vegetables and herbs fresh from the garden or farmer's market.

WHAT YOU NEED

- 2 medium carrots, finely chopped
- 2 stalks celery, finely chopped
- 1 large onion, finely chopped
- 6 cloves garlic, minced
- 1 tablespoon olive oil
- 1 cup water
- 2 pounds tomatoes, chopped (about 6 cups)
- $\frac{1}{2}$ cup snipped fresh basil or 2 tablespoons dried basil, crushed, plus $\frac{1}{2}$ cup snipped fresh parsley
- 1 teaspoon salt
- 1 tablespoon balsamic vinegar

HERE'S HOW

1 In a large saucepan cook carrots, celery, onion, and garlic, covered, in hot oil over medium-low heat for 10 minutes, stirring occasionally. Transfer to a blender container or food processor bowl; add the water. Cover and blend or process until smooth. Return to pan.

2 Stir in half of the tomatoes, half of the fresh basil or all of the dried basil, and the salt. Bring to boiling; reduce heat. Simmer, covered, for 15 minutes. Remove from heat.

3 Stir in the remaining tomatoes, the remaining fresh basil or all of the parsley, and the balsamic vinegar; heat through. Makes 4 servings (6 cups).

Curried Lentil Soup

WHAT YOU NEED

6 cups reduced-sodium chicken broth

1½ cups thinly sliced green onions

2 medium carrots, chopped

1 cup dried brown lentils, rinsed and drained

1 tablespoon grated gingerroot

1 teaspoon curry powder

1 teaspoon ground cumin

⅛ to ¼ teaspoon ground red pepper

¼ cup snipped fresh cilantro

½ cup dairy sour cream (optional)

Fresh cilantro sprigs or green onions (optional)

HERE'S HOW

1 In a large saucepan combine the chicken broth, green onions, carrots, lentils, gingerroot, curry powder, cumin, and red pepper. Bring mixture to boiling; reduce heat. Simmer, covered, for 25 to 30 minutes or until lentils are tender.

2 Stir in the snipped cilantro; cook for 1 minute more. If desired, top each serving with sour cream and garnish with cilantro sprigs. Makes 4 servings (6 cups).

Humble lentils step out in spicy style with a flavor kick of gingerroot, curry powder, cumin, and cilantro. If you like, a spoonful of sour cream swirled into the soup adds complementary richness.

141

Fennel-Asparagus Soup

After playing in the snow, come in for a bowlful of bounty. Small onions, baby carrots, and tender asparagus partner with baby lima beans for this soothing soup.

WHAT YOU NEED

6 cups chicken broth

1 10-ounce package frozen baby lima beans

1 cup small red boiling onions, whole pearl onions, or coarsely chopped onion

1 teaspoon fennel seed, crushed

1/4 teaspoon pepper

1 cup packaged, peeled baby carrots

1 medium fennel bulb

12 ounces asparagus spears, trimmed and cut into 1-inch pieces

4 ounces pancetta, chopped, crisp-cooked, and drained, or 5 slices bacon, crisp-cooked, drained, and crumbled

HERE'S HOW

1 In a Dutch oven combine the chicken broth, lima beans, onions, fennel seed, and pepper. Bring to boiling; reduce heat. Simmer, covered, for 10 minutes. Stir in the carrots and cook for 5 minutes.

2 Meanwhile, cut off and discard upper stalks of fennel, reserving leaves. Snip 1/4 cup fennel leaves; set aside. Remove any wilted outer layers from bulb; cut a thin slice from base. Wash and chop fennel.

3 Stir the chopped fennel, asparagus, and pancetta into Dutch oven. Cook about 5 minutes more or until vegetables are tender. Garnish each serving with the reserved fennel leaves. Makes 4 servings (8 cups).

Warm-Up Soup

Sour cream lends a tangy flavor to this creamy concoction of cheese, asparagus, and potatoes.

WHAT YOU NEED

- 1 large onion, chopped
- 4 teaspoons cooking oil
- 3 tablespoons all-purpose flour
- 2 cups 1-inch pieces asparagus spears or broccoli florets
- 2 cups milk
- 1 14¹/₂-ounce can chicken broth
- 8 ounces red potatoes, cubed (about 1¹/₂ cups)
- ¹/₄ teaspoon salt
- ¹/₈ teaspoon ground red pepper
- 1 cup shredded sharp cheddar cheese (4 ounces)
- 1 small tomato, seeded and chopped
- ¹/₃ cup dairy sour cream

HERE'S HOW

1 In a large saucepan cook onion in hot oil until tender. Sprinkle flour over onion and stir to coat. Add the asparagus, milk, chicken broth, potatoes, salt, and red pepper.

2 Cook and stir until thickened and bubbly; reduce heat. Simmer, covered, for 10 to 12 minutes or until vegetables are just tender, stirring occasionally. Add cheddar cheese, tomato, and sour cream; stir until cheese melts. Makes 4 servings (5¹/₂ cups).

Light The Way

*"A Christmas candle
is a lovely thing;
It makes no noise at all,
But softly gives
itself away;
While quite unselfish,
it grows small."*

—Eva K. Logue

Mirror Images

What You Need

5×7-inch wood picture
  frames; pencil
Small hinges with screws
Drill with small bit
5×7-inch mirrors
Fresh pear and grapes
Tea-light holder and candle
Spoon; white glue
Paintbrush; Epsom salts
Evergreen sprigs
Eucalyptus leaves

Here's How

1   For the mirrored backdrop, remove backing and glass from frames. Hinge frames together in pairs. For each pair, lay frames side by side, right sides down on a flat surface. Place two hinges between frames, marking holes with a pencil. Drill starter holes in frames. Attach hinges with screws. Place mirrors in frames and replace the backings.

2   For candleholder, determine how pear lies best. Invert a metal tea-light holder on top of pear and press down. Remove holder, and spoon out fruit. Dilute glue with water, and brush on pear and grapes; sprinkle with Epsom salts. Insert a tea light into hole and position pear and greenery in front of frames.

For an elegant candleholder, fit a pear with a tea light and embellish it with Epsom salts. Place the fruit candleholder in front of mirrored picture frames to enhance the glow. Complete the display with salt-sprinkled grapes and greenery.

149

Bethlehem Candle

WHAT YOU NEED

Heavy glass cylinder-shape candleholder
Newspapers
Blue glass paint
Tracing paper; pencil
Scissors
Heavy paper
Crafts knife
Tape
Spray adhesive
White spray paint
Decoupage medium
Medium- and fine-liner paintbrushes
White glitter

HERE'S HOW

1 Wash and dry the candleholder. In a well-ventilated work area, place the candleholder on newspapers. Spray two or three light even coats of blue glass paint onto candleholder, allowing to dry between coats.

2 Trace the Bethlehem patterns, *pages 152–153*, onto tracing paper, enlarging or decreasing the size to fit the candleholder if needed. Trace the star pattern onto tracing paper. Cut out the shapes and trace at the bottom of a sheet of heavy paper (the cutout top of the sheet is what you'll tape to the top of the candle so the bottom can be spray-painted white). Cut outline of shape with scissors and cut the window areas and star with a crafts knife.

3 Tape the paper stencil around the jar, leaving the area to be white exposed. Use a small amount of adhesive on small windows to position on jar.

4 Spray the exposed area with white spray paint. Let dry; spray again until well covered. Let dry. Remove paper pattern. Paint in small white dots in sky area. Let dry.

5 With a paintbrush and decoupage medium, paint all white areas. While the decoupage medium is wet, sprinkle with glitter. Let dry. Brush off excess glitter.

Light the way to the manger scene with this easy-to-paint candleholder that displays a glistening silhouette of Bethlehem.

Paper Lanterns

Arrange a cluster of paper lanterns on a table or shelf for an easy, inexpensive way to make a big impact.

NOTE: *Never leave burning candles unattended.*

WHAT YOU NEED

Tracing paper
Pencil
Medium-weight art paper
Crafts knife
Bamboo skewers
Votive candle in clear-glass holder

HERE'S HOW

1 Trace the angel or star pattern, *below.* Christmas coloring books also are good sources for lantern pattern shapes.

2 Cut squares and rectangles from medium-weight art paper. Trace or sketch a design on each paper. Cut out the designs with a crafts knife.

3 Stand each lantern by vertically inserting two bamboo skewers through the back near the top and the bottom. For safety, enclose a candle inside a clear candleholder or drinking glass. Light the candle and set it inside the lantern.

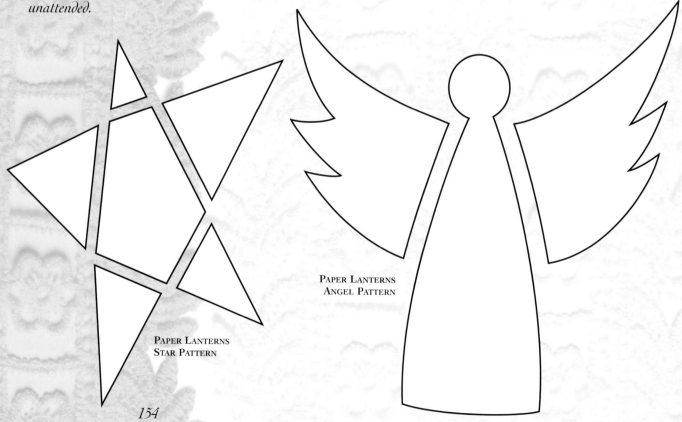

PAPER LANTERNS
STAR PATTERN

PAPER LANTERNS
ANGEL PATTERN

Container Candles

Small containers used as candleholders make striking mantel arrangements or centerpieces when grouped together. Flea markets prove bountiful hunting grounds for vintage egg cups, candy dishes, teacups, bud vases, and tart tins.

WHAT YOU NEED

Clear glass and metal containers, such as egg cups, candy dishes, teacups, bud vases, and tins
Candlemaking kit
Antique ornaments
Ornament hangers

HERE'S HOW

1 Wash and dry containers. Polish metal containers if desired.

2 Fill each container following the instructions with candlemaking kit. Embellish the candleholders with tiny antique ornaments hung from the lip of the container.

Transform ordinary glass ornaments into candleholders that carry the show, whether used solo at place settings or en masse for striking tabletop displays. For extra impact, mix various sizes of clear- and frosted-glass ornaments and stagger heights of candles by cutting them to different lengths.

Ornamental Flair

WHAT YOU NEED

Clear- and frosted-glass ornaments
Scrap wood; pliers
Electric drill, rotary tool, or hammer and nail
Thin taper candles
Metal split ring, such as a key ring

HERE'S HOW

1 Remove metal cap from ornament and discard hanging loop. Turn cap upside down on a piece of scrap wood. Hold cap edge securely with pliers and use an electric drill, rotary tool, or hammer and nail to enlarge the opening to accommodate a thin taper candle. Use caution with power tools.

2 Replace cap on ornament and insert candle through the opening. Place the ornament on a metal split ring, such as a key ring, to keep it upright. Use dripless candles or place ornaments on a tray to avoid wax drips.

Sugared Candles

If you have a sweet tooth for holiday decorating, these whimsical candles and candleholders will fulfill your craving. Use ingredients from the kitchen to decorate fruit, candles, cups, and saucers.

WHAT YOU NEED

Firm fruit
Vegetable peeler
Standard taper candles
Beaten egg whites
Fine sugar
Paintbrush
Tableware
Damp cloth

HERE'S HOW

1 Using a vegetable peeler, bore a hole in fruit the diameter of a standard taper candle; check candle fit. Cover fruit with a wash of beaten egg whites; roll in sugar.

2 Dip a paintbrush in beaten egg whites to make stripes, dots, snowflakes, or other designs on candle and cup. Sprinkle sugar over egg white. Place sugared candles in fruit candleholders, then set in sugared cup, if desired. Use this technique to decorate more candles and tableware.

3 To redo the design, just wipe it off with a damp cloth, let the surface dry, and start over.

Frosted Vase

WHAT YOU NEED

Glass vase
White candles or white candle wax
   (available at crafts stores)
Clean metal can
Saucepan
Waxed paper
Spoon
Unwrapped peppermint disks
Thin taper candle

HERE'S HOW

1 Fill the glass vase with hot water to warm the glass.

2 Cut candles into chunks and remove the wick. Place the wax chunks into the metal can. Never put wax directly in the saucepan. Place the can into a saucepan of hot water on range or electric burner. Heat until the wax melts. Carefully remove the can from the water.

3 Cover the work area with waxed paper. Empty the water from the vase and dry the vase. Drizzle melted wax over the vase with a spoon. Allow the wax to harden.

4 Place a base of peppermint disks in the vase. Stand a candle on the disks and fill the vase around the candle with additional candy disks.

White-as-snow wax lends a wintry touch to an ordinary clear-glass vase. Fill the vase with peppermints for ready-for-the-holidays flair.

Mantel Magic

What You Need

White glue
Paintbrush
Epsom salts
Metallic embroidery floss
Snowflake charms
Gold fine-gauge wire
Wire cutter
Clear, white, or
  frosted beads

Here's How

1 For a snowy effect, brush white glue over an entire candle or use it to paint a design, such as a snowflake. Sprinkle candle with, or roll it in, Epsom salts.

2 For a floss-trimmed candle, separate plies of metallic embroidery floss and wrap it around the candle in random patterns. For extra trim, thread several snowflake charms onto floss before wrapping.

3 For bead-trimmed candles, cut gold fine-gauge beading wire into 1-inch-long pieces. Thread wire through a bead, bend wire into a U-shape, and press ends into the candle to cover the candle in beads.

For high style at a fraction of the cost, embellish everyday candles with items retrieved from drawers and cupboards. Clear beads, wisps of metallic embroidery floss, thin gold wire, and snow-like Epsom salts add texture and design.

Star Candlesticks

Star candle wraps set the stage for this luminous table setting. Wire curlicues, small star mirrors, and glass beads enhance the candlelight.

WHAT YOU NEED

24-gauge wire; wire cutters
Gold spray paint
Glass candlesticks
White crafts glue or hot-glue gun and hot-glue sticks
Pencil; glass beads
Small star-shape mirrors (available at crafts stores)

HERE'S HOW

1 Cut wire into various lengths. Paint some wires gold; leave others silver.

2 Wrap wire around the base of each candlestick in a spontaneous pattern. Wrap wires that extend from the candlestick around a pencil to create spirals. String beads onto spirals and glue others in place. Glue on star-shape mirrors.

Instead of standing candles solo in soldier-straight rows, casually group them like fresh-cut flowers in a vase. Use sand or aquarium gravel to anchor the candle bouquet in a decorative glass urn.

$\mathcal{C}$andle $\mathcal{B}$ouquet

WHAT YOU NEED

Wide-mouth glass container or vase
Sand or aquarium gravel
Dripless taper candles

HERE'S HOW

1 Wash and dry the glass container or vase. Fill the bottom one-third with sand or gravel.

2 Arrange a grouping of dripless taper candles in the sand, allowing the candles to fall playfully to the side, resting on the container edge.

Canning Jar Luminarias

What You Need

Canning jars
**Colorful, nonflammable
items, such as buttons,
candy, marbles, and
aquarium rocks**
Votive candle
Votive cup

Here's How

1 Wash and dry the canning
jars. Fill jars one-half to
two-thirds full of colorful
nonflammable items.

2 Place a candle in a votive
cup and nestle it in the
center of the jar.

*Place
nonflammable
items in holiday
colors in
transparent
canning jars.
Use alone or
group together.
These candles
will be the
subject of
conversation
at your next
holiday
gathering.*

$\mathcal{S}$parkling $\mathcal{B}$eaded $\mathcal{C}$andle

Light dances through vibrant color on this easy-to-make beaded candleholder. Shop at a favorite crafts store for the beads or scout flea markets for glass-bead necklaces.

WHAT YOU NEED

Beading wire; wire cutters; glass or plastic beads
Glass votive candleholder
Hot-glue gun; hot-glue sticks

HERE'S HOW

1 Cut a piece of wire approximately 36 inches long. Place one bead on the end of the wire; thread the wire through the bead a second time to secure. String beads on wire, securing the last bead as for the first.

2 Wrap beaded wire around candleholder to determine placement. If a longer length is desired, cut and bead an extra length of wire. Secure one end of beaded wire with glue at the top edge of the candleholder. Wrap the beaded wire around the candleholder, securing with glue about every 1 inch.

Wire Mesh Candles

WHAT YOU NEED

Votive candleholder, juice glass, or bud vase
Wire mesh (available by the foot at hardware stores)
Wire cutters
Beads
Fine-gauge aluminum wire
Colored wire
Strong adhesive, such as E6000
Candles

HERE'S HOW

1 Wrap the vessel with wire mesh.

2 Measure vessel dimensions and cut with wire cutters, leaving spikes along seam for closure and four evenly spaced spikes along bottom for feet. Fold up remaining spikes to hold vessel.

3 Adorn mesh with beads attached with aluminum wire. Or shape a piece of colored wire in a holiday phrase and attach it to mesh.

4 Glue beads to bottom spikes for feet. Insert candles.

Bring contemporary style to your Christmas table with sleek candle covers made of wire mesh. Use the photograph, below, for inspiration and have fun creating your own designs.

Carved-Diamonds Candle

Nestled in the center of a plate of vintage ornaments, this elegant candle is carved, then painted with glistening gold-tone flecks.

WHAT YOU NEED

Pencil
Purchased red pillar candle
Linoleum carving cutter tool (available at art and crafts stores)
Gold acrylic paint; paintbrush
Fine gold glitter

HERE'S HOW

1 Use a pencil to mark dots approximately ½ inch apart around the top and bottom of the candle.

2 Connect dots diagonally around the candle from top to bottom, using the linoleum carving cutter. Shake off the wax from the cutter as it builds. *Note: Linoleum cutters are very sharp. Always work AWAY from your hands and face.*

3 After the design is completed, paint the carved crevices as shown in Photo 1, *below.*

4 Rub the paint into the crevices as shown in Photo 2. While the paint is wet, sprinkle with glitter. Let dry.

Candies
Oh-So-Sweet

"Christmas is the season for kindling the fire of hospitality in the hall, the genial flame of charity in the heart."

—Washington Irving

Peanut Butter Fudge

Chopped peanuts and a hint of chocolate top these sweet wedges of fudge. Lining the pan with foil ahead of time makes it easy to get the fudge out after it sets.

WHAT YOU NEED

Butter
4 cups granulated sugar
2 5-ounce cans (1⅓ cups total) evaporated milk
1 cup butter
1 12-ounce package (2 cups) peanut-butter-flavor pieces
1 7-ounce jar marshmallow crème
1 cup chopped peanuts
1 teaspoon vanilla
Whole or coarsely chopped peanuts (optional)
½ cup semisweet chocolate pieces
1 teaspoon shortening

HERE'S HOW

1 Line a 13×9×2-inch baking pan with foil, extending foil over edges of pan. Butter foil; set aside.

2 Butter sides of a heavy 3-quart saucepan. Combine sugar, evaporated milk, and 1 cup butter in buttered saucepan. Cook and stir over medium-high heat until mixture boils. Reduce heat to medium; continue cooking and stirring for 10 minutes.

3 Remove pan from heat. Add peanut-butter-flavor pieces, marshmallow crème, peanuts, and vanilla; stir until peanut-butter-flavor pieces are melted and mixture is combined. Beat by hand for 5 to 8 minutes or until mixture becomes very thick and just starts to lose its gloss. Spread in prepared pan.

4 When fudge is firm, use foil to lift it out of pan. Cut fudge into 1-inch triangles or squares. Cool completely. Sprinkle with whole or chopped peanuts, if desired. Melt semisweet chocolate pieces and shortening in a small saucepan over low heat. Drizzle over top of fudge. Store in a tightly covered container in the refrigerator. Makes about 4 pounds (96 pieces).

Cappuccino Caramels

WHAT YOU NEED

Butter

- 1 cup butter or margarine
- 1 16-ounce package (2¼ cups packed) brown sugar
- 1 14-ounce can sweetened condensed milk (1¼ cups)
- 1 cup light corn syrup
- 3 tablespoons instant coffee crystals
- 1 cup chopped walnuts
- 1 teaspoon vanilla
- ½ to 1 teaspoon finely shredded orange peel

A great make-ahead candy to give or enjoy, these chewy caramels store for up to nine months in the freezer.

HERE'S HOW

1 Line a 9×9×2-inch baking pan with foil, extending the foil over edges of pan. Grease the foil with butter; set the pan aside.

2 In a heavy 3-quart saucepan melt 1 cup butter over low heat. Stir in the brown sugar, sweetened condensed milk, corn syrup, and instant coffee crystals. Carefully clip a candy thermometer to the side of the pan.

3 Cook over medium heat, stirring constantly, until the thermometer registers 248°F or candy reaches firm-ball stage. The mixture should boil at a moderate, steady rate over the entire surface. Reaching firm-ball stage should take 15 to 20 minutes.

4 Remove the saucepan from the heat. Remove the candy thermometer from the saucepan. Immediately stir in walnuts, vanilla, and orange peel. Pour the caramel mixture into the prepared baking pan, smoothing the surface; cool.

5 When caramel is firm, use the foil to lift it out of the pan. Use a buttered knife to cut the caramel into squares.

6 Wrap each caramel square in plastic wrap. Or place caramel squares in candy cups; arrange in a box lined with cellophane or in a tin. Makes 64 pieces (about 3 pounds).

Holiday Sweets

This assortment of candies will please everyone in the house. The recipes for Caramel-Nut Corn, Marbled Pecan Bark, Peanutty Fudge Log, Raspberry Truffles, Pretzel-Candy Crunch, Even-More-Remarkable Fudge, Almond-Butter Crunch, and Rum-Raisin Clusters begin on page 180.

2 Remove saucepan from heat. Add marshmallows, chocolate pieces, butterscotch pieces, the ½ cup chopped peanuts, and vanilla. Stir until marshmallows melt. Chill, if necessary, until firm enough to handle.

3 Shape mixture into a 15×2-inch log. Roll in finely chopped peanuts. Chill; cut into ½-inch slices. Store tightly covered in the refrigerator. Makes 30 slices (about 1½ pounds).

Raspberry Truffles

Divinely rich and creamy, these truffles have delightful berry flavor.

WHAT YOU NEED

½ cup seedless raspberry preserves
2 tablespoons raspberry liqueur
8 ounces semisweet chocolate
6 tablespoons butter (no substitutes)
10 ounces chocolate-flavor and/or vanilla-flavor candy coating, cut up
Rolled fondant ribbons, candied violets, melted vanilla-flavor candy coating (optional)

HERE'S HOW

1 Combine preserves and liqueur in a blender container or food processor bowl. Blend or process until smooth. Melt chocolate and butter in a heavy medium saucepan. Cool to room temperature.

2 Whisk raspberry puree into chocolate mixture. Pour into a shallow bowl; refrigerate 3 hours or until firm. Shape into 1-inch balls. Chill until firm.

3 Melt candy coating in a heavy saucepan over low heat. Cool slightly. Dip each chocolate ball into melted coating. Place on a tray lined with waxed paper. If desired, decorate tops with fondant ribbons, candied violets, or drizzled candy coating. Store in an airtight container in the refrigerator. Makes about 30.

Pretzel-Candy Crunch

WHAT YOU NEED

    2 cups broken pretzels
    1 cup tiny marshmallows
    1/2 cup chopped salted cashews or peanuts
    3/4 cup sugar
    1/3 cup half-and-half or light cream
    2 tablespoons butter or margarine
    1 cup butterscotch-flavor pieces

HERE'S HOW

1 Combine pretzels, marshmallows, and cashews or peanuts in a large mixing bowl; set aside. Combine sugar, half-and-half or light cream, and butter or margarine in a heavy saucepan. Bring to boiling over medium heat, stirring constantly. Add butterscotch pieces. Let stand 1 minute to soften pieces. Stir until combined. Let stand 5 minutes. Remove from heat.

2 Pour butterscotch mixture over pretzel mixture; stir to coat. Drop by rounded teaspoons onto baking sheets lined with waxed paper. Chill until firm. Store in a tightly covered container in the refrigerator. Makes about 30.

These clusters carry the candy-coated pretzel idea one step further with the addition of marshmallows and peanuts.

Even-More-Remarkable Fudge

WHAT YOU NEED

      Butter
    4 cups sugar
    2 5-ounce cans (1 1/3 cups total) evaporated milk
    1 cup butter (no substitutes)
    1 12-ounce package (2 cups) semisweet chocolate pieces
    1 7-ounce dark chocolate or milk chocolate candy
        bar, cut up
    1 7-ounce jar marshmallow crème
    1 cup chopped walnuts
    1 teaspoon vanilla

Holiday Sweets instructions are continued on page 184.

A candy bar adds more rich chocolate flavor to this remarkable easy-to-make fudge.

Holiday Sweets

HERE'S HOW

1 Line a 13×9×2-inch baking pan with foil, extending foil over edges of pan. Butter foil; set aside.

2 Butter sides of a heavy 3-quart saucepan. In saucepan, combine sugar, evaporated milk, and the 1 cup butter. Cook and stir over medium-high heat until mixture boils. Reduce heat to medium and continue cooking and stirring for 10 minutes.

3 Remove pan from heat. Add the chocolate pieces, cut-up chocolate bar, marshmallow crème, walnuts, and vanilla; stir until chocolate melts and mixture is combined. Beat by hand for 1 minute. Spread in the prepared pan. Score into 1-inch squares while warm. When fudge is firm, use foil to lift it out of pan. Cut fudge into squares. Store in a tightly covered container in the refrigerator. Makes 96 pieces (4 pounds).

Almond-Butter Crunch

This candy delivers superb taste with just four ingredients.

WHAT YOU NEED

Butter
1 **cup slivered almonds**
1/2 **cup butter (no substitutes)**
1/2 **cup sugar**
1 **tablespoon light corn syrup**

HERE'S HOW

1 Line bottom and sides of a 9-inch round baking pan (do not use a glass pan) with foil. Butter the foil heavily. Set pan aside.

2 Combine almonds, the 1/2 cup butter, sugar, and syrup in a 10-inch skillet. Cook over medium heat until sugar is melted and mixture turns golden brown, stirring constantly (about 10 minutes).

3 Quickly spread mixture into prepared pan. Cool about 15 minutes or until firm. Remove candy by lifting edges of foil. Peel off foil. Cool. Leave candy as a single disk or break into pieces. Makes about ¾ pound (15 servings).

Rum-Raisin Clusters

WHAT YOU NEED

1	6-ounce package (1 cup) semisweet chocolate pieces
¼	cup whipping cream
1	tablespoon rum
1½	cups raisins
½	cup chopped pecans
2	ounces white baking bar

HERE'S HOW

1 Combine chocolate pieces and whipping cream in a small saucepan. Cook and stir over low heat until chocolate melts and mixture is smooth. Stir in rum until smooth. Stir in raisins and pecans.

2 Drop spoonfuls of chocolate mixture into 1-inch paper candy cups. In another small saucepan melt white baking bar over low heat, stirring constantly; drizzle over raisin clusters. Chill until firm. Store in a tightly covered container in the refrigerator. Makes about 36 pieces.

If you don't have candy cups, drop spoonfuls of the raisin mixture onto a baking sheet lined with waxed paper.

185

Nutty Bars

Combine creamy, smooth marshmallow centers and peanuts for these tasty Salted Peanut Bars. The Pecan Clusters are irresistible combinations of nuts, chocolate, and caramel.

Salted Peanut Bars

WHAT YOU NEED

Nonstick cooking spray
4 cups dry-roasted or honey-roasted peanuts
1/2 cup butter
1 10$^1/_2$-ounce package tiny marshmallows
1 12-ounce package peanut-butter-flavor pieces
1 14-ounce can (1$^1/_4$ cups) sweetened condensed milk
1/2 cup creamy peanut butter

HERE'S HOW

1 Line a 13×9×2-inch baking pan with heavy foil. Spray foil with cooking spray. Spread half of the nuts over the pan.

2 In a 3-quart saucepan, melt butter with marshmallows over low heat. Stir in peanut butter pieces, condensed milk, and peanut butter until smooth. Quickly pour over the nuts in pan. Sprinkle remaining nuts on top.

3 Chill; cut into pieces. Store in refrigerator. Makes 48 pieces.

Chocolate-Caramel Pecan Clusters

WHAT YOU NEED

4$^1/_2$ cups pecan halves (1 pound)
2 cups sugar
2 cups whipping cream
$^3/_4$ cup light-colored corn syrup
1/2 cup butter
1/8 teaspoon salt
1$^1/_3$ cups semisweet chocolate pieces
1$^1/_3$ cups white baking pieces
2 teaspoons shortening

HERE'S HOW

1 Preheat oven to 350°F. In a shallow baking pan, spread pecan halves in a thin layer. Bake in the preheated oven

for 5 to 10 minutes or until pecans are light brown, stirring once or twice. Cool in pan on a wire rack.

2 Line several baking sheets with foil; grease foil. Arrange pecans in 20 groups, 3½ inches apart, on the baking sheets.

3 In a 3-quart saucepan, mix sugar, 1½ cups of the whipping cream, corn syrup, butter, and salt. Cook and stir over medium-high heat to boiling.

4 With mixture boiling, very slowly add the remaining ½ cup whipping cream. Clip a candy thermometer to side of pan. Reduce heat to medium-low. (Mixture should boil at a moderate rate over entire surface.)

5 Cook, stirring occasionally, until mixture reaches 244°F (firm-ball stage). Don't allow mixture to boil over. Remove from heat immediately. Remove candy thermometer. Pour into a 4-cup glass measuring cup.

6 Quickly pour half of the caramel mixture over pecans. (If it is very hot, it will run more. Push caramel back to pecan mound with a small spatula.) Repeat with remaining caramel mixture. (It will have cooled enough to mound.)

7 In a small saucepan, melt 1 cup of the chocolate pieces over low heat. In another saucepan, melt 1 cup of the white baking pieces over low heat. Spread half of the caramel mounds with melted chocolate and half with melted white baking pieces.

8 Using the same saucepans, melt the remaining ⅓ cup chocolate pieces and 1 teaspoon of the shortening in one saucepan and the remaining ⅓ cup white baking pieces and the remaining 1 teaspoon shortening in the other.

9 Drizzle the chocolate over white-frosted candies; drizzle the white over the chocolate-frosted candies. Use a toothpick to swirl the drizzle. Let stand until set. Store in the refrigerator. Makes 20 candies.

Candied Citrus Peels

WHAT YOU NEED

2 medium oranges, lemons, or limes or
    4 medium tangerines
$1^{1}/_{3}$ cups sugar
    Additional sugar (about $^{1}/_{4}$ cup)

HERE'S HOW

1 Cut the peels of the fruit into quarters, cutting through peels to the pulp. Loosen peel from the pulp with a spoon as shown, *below right*, leaving white membrane attached to the peel. (Reserve pulp for another use.)

2 Place the fruit peel in a 2-quart nonmetal bowl. Add enough cold water to cover. If necessary, place a plate in the bowl to keep the fruit peel submerged. Let stand overnight.

3 Drain the peel. Rinse with cold water. Place peel in a 2-quart saucepan. Cover with cold water. Bring to boiling, then drain. Boil and drain the peel three more times. Cool thoroughly.

4 Cut the peel into $^{1}/_{8}$- to $^{1}/_{4}$-inch-wide strips. Combine the $1^{1}/_{3}$ cups sugar and $^{1}/_{3}$ cup water in a medium saucepan. Bring to boiling, stirring constantly to dissolve sugar. Add the peel. Return to boiling; reduce heat and cook over medium-low heat for 15 to 20 minutes, stirring occasionally, until peel is almost translucent. Do not overcook.

5 Remove peel from syrup using a slotted spoon, and place on a wire rack over waxed paper. Discard syrup. Cool until lukewarm. While peel is still slightly sticky, roll in sugar to coat. Dry on the rack for 1 to 2 hours. Tightly cover and store in a cool, dry place for up to 1 week or in the freezer for up to 6 months. Makes about 2 cups.

Delight the baker on your Christmas list with homemade sugared citrus peels. These plump beauties are luscious in fruitcakes, cookies, and sweet breads.

Sweet Bites

With just a few ingredients you can make Prancer's Penuche even when time is short. For a candy-coated treat, try a nut-cereal-marshmallow mix that's always a holiday favorite.

Prancer's Penuche

WHAT YOU NEED

   Butter
2 **cups packed light brown sugar**
$^2/_3$ **cup milk**
   Dash salt
1 **cup chopped walnuts or sliced almonds**

HERE'S HOW

1 Line a baking sheet with foil; butter the foil.

2 Butter the sides of a heavy 2-quart saucepan. In saucepan, combine brown sugar, milk, and salt. Cook over medium-high heat for about 5 minutes or until boiling, stirring constantly with a wooden spoon. (Avoid splashing mixture on side of pan.) Carefully clip candy thermometer to side of pan.

3 Cook over medium-low heat, stirring frequently, for 18 to 20 minutes or until mixture reaches 236°F (soft-ball stage). Remove from heat. Cool without stirring for 50 minutes or until mixture is lukewarm (110°F).

4 Remove candy thermometer. Beat candy vigorously with a wooden spoon until mixture just begins to thicken. Add nuts. Continue beating until candy is very thick and just starts to lose its gloss (about 10 minutes total). Quickly turn onto prepared baking sheet. Let stand for 45 to 60 minutes. Cut into pieces. Store tightly covered. Makes about 1 pound.

Mom's White Chocolate Candy

WHAT YOU NEED

$1^1/_4$ **pounds vanilla-flavor candy coating or almond bark, cut up**
$1^1/_2$ **cups tiny red and green marshmallows**
$1^1/_2$ **cups peanut butter cereal**
$1^1/_2$ **cups crisp rice cereal**
$1^1/_2$ **cups mixed nuts**

HERE'S HOW

1 In a baking dish, heat candy coating in a 200°F oven for 25 minutes or until melted; stir occasionally.

2 In a large bowl, combine marshmallows, cereals, and nuts. Pour melted coating over mixture; stir to coat.

3 Drop mixture by rounded teaspoons onto waxed-paper-lined baking sheets.* Let stand until candy is set. Makes about 40 pieces.

* NOTE: *If you like, pat candy into a buttered 13×9×2-inch baking pan. Once set, cut into squares.*

Festive Fudge Bars

Choose a buttercream topping — cherry, chocolate-mint, or maple-nut — to crown this exquisite milk chocolate confection.

WHAT YOU NEED

Butter
1 16-ounce package (4 cups) powdered sugar
½ cup unsweetened cocoa powder
½ cup butter
⅓ cup water
½ cup nonfat dry milk powder
Cherry, Chocolate-Mint, or Maple-Nut Toppers

HERE'S HOW

1 Line a 13×9×2-inch baking pan with foil, extending foil over edges of pan. Butter foil; set aside.

2 Sift together the powdered sugar and cocoa powder in a large mixing bowl. (If mixture seems lumpy, sift again.) Set aside.

3 Heat the ½ cup butter and the water in a saucepan just to boiling, stirring to melt butter. Stir in dry milk powder. Add butter mixture to powdered sugar mixture; stir until well combined. Spread fudge mixture in prepared pan. Chill in refrigerator while preparing desired topper.

4 Spread topper over fudge. Chill several hours. Use foil to lift fudge out of pan. Cut into shapes. Refrigerate the leftover fudge.

5 CHERRY TOPPER: Beat ⅓ cup softened butter with an electric mixer on medium speed until fluffy. Add 1¾ cups powdered sugar; beat until smooth. Beat in 3 tablespoons milk. Beat in 1¾ cups more powdered sugar and several drops of red food coloring. Stir in ¼ cup finely chopped red candied cherries. Spread over chocolate fudge layer. Chill several hours.

6 CHOCOLATE-MINT TOPPER: Prepare as for Cherry Topper, except add ½ teaspoon mint extract to the butter mixture, omit cherries, and use green food coloring instead of red. Spread over the chocolate fudge layer, then melt ½ cup semisweet chocolate pieces with 1 teaspoon shortening; drizzle mixture over mint topping. Chill several hours.

7 MAPLE-NUT TOPPER: Prepare as for Cherry Topper, except omit the 3 tablespoons milk, the red food coloring, and candied cherries. Beat ⅓ cup maple or maple-flavor syrup into the butter mixture. Add milk, 1 tablespoon at a time, to slightly thin the mixture, if necessary. Spread over chocolate fudge layer. Sprinkle with ½ cup toasted pecan pieces. Chill for several hours. Makes about 2 pounds.

Coffee-Pecan Toffee

WHAT YOU NEED

Butter
2 cups butter (no substitutes)
2 cups sugar
2 tablespoons mild-flavor molasses
1 tablespoon instant espresso powder
2 teaspoons vanilla
3 tablespoons butter (no substitutes)
1 teaspoon instant espresso powder
2 cups semisweet chocolate pieces
1½ cups finely chopped, toasted pecans

HERE'S HOW

1 Line a 15×10×1-inch baking pan with foil, extending foil over edges of pan. Set pan aside. Butter the sides of a heavy 3-quart saucepan. Melt the 2 cups butter in saucepan. Add sugar, ⅓ cup water, molasses, and the 1 tablespoon espresso powder. Cook and stir over medium-high heat until mixture boils.

2 Clip a candy thermometer to side of pan. Reduce heat to medium; continue boiling at a moderate steady rate, stirring frequently, until thermometer registers 290°F, soft-crack stage (about 25 minutes). Watch carefully after 280°F to prevent scorching.

3 Remove saucepan from heat; remove thermometer. Stir in vanilla. Pour candy into the prepared pan. Let candy stand about 1 hour or until firm. Use foil to lift candy out of pan. Break candy into approximately 2-inch-square pieces.

4 Melt the 3 tablespoons butter in a heavy medium saucepan. Stir in the 1 teaspoon espresso powder until dissolved. Add chocolate pieces and melt over low heat, stirring often.

5 Dip half of each candy piece into melted chocolate mixture, coating all sides. Place dipped candy on waxed paper. Sprinkle with pecans. Chill until chocolate is firm. Store in a tightly covered container. Makes about 2¾ pounds (about 48 pieces).

This can't-eat-just-one candy contains a large amount of butter, which will prevent it from sticking to the unbuttered foil. Share it with holiday guests to make their visits unforgettable.

Nutty Chews

These holiday candies will disappear quickly, so be sure to make an extra batch or two.

Caramel Snappers

WHAT YOU NEED

1½ cups pecan halves
    Butter
½ of 14-ounce package vanilla caramels
    (about 25 caramels)
1 tablespoon water
½ cup semisweet chocolate pieces

HERE'S HOW

1 Spread nuts in single layer in a shallow baking pan. Toast in a 350°F oven about 10 minutes, stirring occasionally. Line baking sheet with foil; butter foil. On prepared baking sheet arrange toasted pecan halves in groups of 3, placing flat sides down; set aside. In a heavy 1-quart saucepan combine caramels and water. Cook over low heat, stirring constantly, until caramels are melted and smooth. Remove from heat. Drop about 1 teaspoon caramel mixture onto each group of pecans. Let stand 20 minutes or until caramel mixture is firm.

2 In a saucepan heat chocolate pieces over low heat, stirring constantly, until melted and smooth. Remove from heat. Spread small amount of chocolate over each caramel center. Let stand until firm. Store tightly covered. Makes 30 pieces.

Honey and Macadamia-Nut Fudge

WHAT YOU NEED

    Butter
1½ cups granulated sugar
1 cup packed brown sugar
⅓ cup half-and-half or light cream
⅓ cup milk
2 tablespoons honey
2 tablespoons butter
1 teaspoon vanilla
½ cup toasted macadamia nuts, hazelnuts, or pecans, chopped

HERE'S HOW

1 Line an 8×8×2-inch baking pan with foil, extending foil over edges; set aside.

2 Butter sides of a heavy 2-quart saucepan. In saucepan combine sugars, half-and-half, milk, and honey. Bring to boiling over medium-high heat, stirring constantly with a wooden spoon to dissolve sugars (about 5 minutes). Avoid splashing mixture on sides of pan. Carefully clip candy thermometer to pan.

3 Cook over medium-low heat, stirring frequently, until thermometer registers 236°F, soft-ball stage (10 to 12 minutes). Mixture should boil at a moderate, steady rate over entire surface. Remove from heat. Add the 2 tablespoons butter and vanilla, but do not stir. Cool about 50 minutes, without stirring, to lukewarm, 110°F. Remove thermometer from pan.

4 Beat vigorously with wooden spoon until mixture just begins to thicken; add chopped nuts. Continue beating about 10 minutes until mixture is very thick and just starts to lose its gloss. Quickly turn into prepared pan. While mixture is warm, score into 1¼-inch squares. Use foil to lift candy out of pan when firm; cut into squares. Store in tightly covered container. Makes 36 pieces.

Christmas Gumdrops

Children will be all smiles when they see these colorful confections awaiting.

WHAT YOU NEED

Butter
1 cup sugar
1 cup light corn syrup
3/4 cup water
1 3/4-ounce package powdered fruit pectin
1/2 teaspoon baking soda
Sugar

HERE'S HOW

1 Line a 9×5×3-inch loaf pan with foil, extending foil over edges. Butter foil; set aside. Butter sides of a heavy 1½-quart saucepan. In saucepan combine the 1 cup sugar and corn syrup. Cook over medium-high heat to boiling, stirring constantly with a wooden spoon until sugar dissolves (about 10 minutes). Avoid splashing mixture on sides of pan. Carefully clip candy thermometer to side of pan. Cook over medium-high heat, stirring occasionally, until thermometer registers 280°F, soft-crack stage (about 10 minutes). Mixture should boil at a moderate, steady rate over the entire surface.

2 Meanwhile, in a heavy 2-quart saucepan, combine water, pectin, and baking soda. Mixture will be foamy. Cook over high heat to boiling, stirring constantly (about 2 minutes). Remove from heat; set aside.

3 When sugar mixture reaches soft-crack stage, remove from heat; remove thermometer. Return pectin mixture to high heat; cook until mixture just begins to simmer. Gradually pour hot sugar mixture in thin stream (slightly less than ⅛-inch diameter) into boiling pectin mixture, stirring constantly, for 1 to 2 minutes. Cook, stirring constantly, 1 minute more.

4 Remove saucepan from heat. Add desired flavoring and coloring (see variations *opposite*). Pour mixture into prepared pan. Let stand 2 hours or until firm. Use foil to lift candy out of pan. Using a buttered knife, cut candy into ¾-inch squares. Roll in sugar. Store loosely covered. Makes about 72 pieces.

5 **Orange Gumdrops:** Add 1½ teaspoons orange extract, 1 teaspoon finely shredded orange peel, 4 drops yellow food coloring, and 1 drop red food coloring. Continue as directed.

6 **Cinnamon Gumdrops:** Add 3 drops oil of cinnamon and 7 drops red food coloring. Continue as directed.

7 **Mint Gumdrops:** Add ¾ teaspoon mint extract and 7 drops green food coloring. Continue as directed.

8 **Lemon Gumdrops:** Add 1½ teaspoons lemon extract, 1 teaspoon finely shredded lemon peel, and 7 drops yellow food coloring. Continue as directed.

Christmas Crunch

Need a quick candy for a bake sale? These rich no-bake treats are sure to be popular. Kids will want to help make these rich and gooey treats. Reserve some of the crushed peppermint candies to press into the candy coating mixture after spreading it on the baking sheet.

Butterscotch Bites

WHAT YOU NEED

6	tablespoons butter (no substitutes), melted
1	cup creamy peanut butter
1$^{1}/_2$	cups sifted powdered sugar
1	9-ounce package chocolate wafers, crushed
1	10- to 11-ounce package (2 cups) butterscotch-flavor pieces
$^1/_4$	cup whipping cream
$^3/_4$	cup chopped peanuts

HERE'S HOW

1 For chocolate layer, stir together butter, peanut butter, and powdered sugar in a large mixing bowl. Stir in crushed chocolate wafers. Combine well. Press mixture into the bottom of a 13×9×2-inch baking pan.

2 For butterscotch layer, combine butterscotch pieces and whipping cream in a heavy small saucepan. Stir over low heat until pieces are melted. Carefully spoon and spread butterscotch mixture over chocolate mixture. Sprinkle chopped peanuts over butterscotch mixture. Chill at least 2 hours. Cut candy into 1-inch squares to serve. Cover and store in refrigerator. Makes 96.

White Chocolate Clusters

WHAT YOU NEED

1$^{1}/_4$	pounds vanilla-flavor candy coating or almond bark, cut up
1$^{1}/_2$	cups tiny marshmallows
1$^{1}/_2$	cups peanut butter cereal
1$^{1}/_2$	cups crisp rice cereal
1$^{1}/_2$	cups mixed nuts

1 Heat candy coating or almond bark in a heavy 2-quart saucepan over low heat, stirring constantly until melted and smooth. Remove from heat.

2 Combine marshmallows, cereals, and nuts in a large bowl. Pour melted coating over mixture; stir to coat. Drop mixture by rounded teaspoons onto baking sheets lined with waxed paper. Let stand until candy is set. Makes about 40.

Peppermint Crunch Candies

WHAT YOU NEED

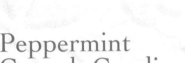

1 pound vanilla-flavor candy coating, cut up
3/4 cup finely crushed hard peppermint candies
Few drops red or green food coloring

HERE'S HOW

1 Line a baking sheet with foil; set aside. Heat candy coating in a heavy 2-quart saucepan over low heat, stirring constantly until melted and smooth. Remove from heat. Stir in crushed candies and food coloring. Pour candy-coating mixture onto the prepared baking sheet. Spread to about ⅜-inch thickness.

2 Chill candy about 30 minutes or until firm. (Or let candy stand at room temperature several hours or until firm.) Use foil to lift firm candy from the baking sheet; carefully break candy into pieces. Store tightly covered up to 2 weeks. Makes about 1 pound or 20 pieces.

Decorating
Indoors & Out

〰

"Happy, happy Christmas, that can win us back to the delusions of our childhood days, recall to the old man the pleasures of his youth, and transport the traveler back to his own fireside and quiet home!"

—Charles Dickens

〰

Ever-Bright Branches

WHAT YOU NEED FOR THE GARLAND

Wide white satin wired ribbon on a spool; scissors
Pencil; fabric paints in purple, turquoise, green, and red
2 wood beads with wide openings for each banner
Acrylic paints in purple, turquoise, green, and red
Paintbrush

WHAT YOU NEED FOR THE ORNAMENTS

Tracing paper; pencil; scissors; ⅛-inch-thick craft foam
Spray adhesive; metallic papers; utility knife
White fabric paint; white glitter; paper punch

HERE'S HOW

1 **For garland,** unwind a spool of wide white ribbon. Using a pencil, lightly write phrases, *page 208.* Allow approximately 6 to 12 inches of blank space on both sides of the writing. Fold the ribbon in half lengthwise and cut a V-shape into each ribbon end, cutting from the fold outward to the end. Trace the phrases with fabric paint. Let dry.

2 Place the beads onto a paintbrush handle so that you can hold it easily while painting. Use acrylic paints to paint base coats. Let dry. Paint dots by dipping the handle end of a paintbrush into paint and dotting onto the painted bead.

3 **For ornaments,** trace the patterns, *pages 206–207,* onto tracing paper and cut out.

4 In a well-ventilated work area, spray the back side of metallic paper with a heavy coat of spray adhesive. Apply to white craft foam.

5 Trace shapes onto foamed metallic paper and cut out with a utility knife. For shapes with two colors, such as gift package, cut the second color from paper only and apply adhesive to back side. Attach to the ornament.

6 Outline the shapes with white fabric paint and sprinkle with white glitter before the paint dries. Let dry. Shake off excess glitter. Using a paper punch, punch hole in ornament and loop a ribbon through for hanging.

These playful ornaments and garlands will awaken childhood memories of magical Christmases past.

EVER-BRIGHT BRANCHES
ORNAMENT PATTERNS

EVER-BRIGHT BRANCHES
ORNAMENT PATTERNS

Twas the night before Christmas

When all through the house

Not a creature was stirring

not even a mouse

EVER-BRIGHT BRANCHES
GARLAND PATTERNS

1 SQUARE = 1 INCH

EVER-BRIGHT BRANCHES
ORNAMENT PATTERN

Precious tabletop Christmas trees make wonderful place-setting decorations, hostess gifts, or your next dinner party favor.

Tabletop Tree

WHAT YOU NEED

Florist's foam; scissors or knife
Small silver containers
Several 6- to 8-inch sprigs of greenery for each
Epsom salts; earring wires; beads

HERE'S HOW

1 For each tree, cut florist's foam into a cube that almost fills the silver container. Place the foam in the container.

2 Trim greenery sprigs to desired lengths. Push the end of each sprig into the center of the foam. Add water.

3 Pour Epsom salts into the container to cover the foam for a snowy-looking base.

4 Thread beads onto wires and hang them on the tree.

Heavenly Angel

This elegant angel is made of paper and accented with wood, lace, and a button. Place her on top of the tree to watch over you all Christmas season.

WHAT YOU NEED

Tracing paper
Pencil
Scissors
Heavy-textured decorative paper
Wood ring
White pearl acrylic paint
Paintbrush and water
Hot-glue gun; hot-glue sticks
Narrow braid trim
Lace trim for the bottom
Large pearl button for head
Pearls

HERE'S HOW

1 Trace the patterns, *pages 212–213,* onto tracing paper. Cut out the patterns and trace onto decorative paper. Cut out all pieces.

2 Paint the wood ring white and set aside to dry.

3 Referring to the patterns, make all the folds in the dress piece.

4 Using the photograph, *opposite,* as a guide, glue the lace trim to the two bottom sides of rectangle piece. Glue the narrow braid trim to the top sides of the dress and the inside edge of the large angel wings.

5 Fold the narrow end of the dress over just enough to loop around the wood ring and glue in place. Glue the starburst paper piece onto the ring.

6 Shape the wings and flowers, pulling and curling to shape the petals to curve outward and the wings to curve upward. To coil the paper, shape it around a pencil or other round object.

7 Glue the small wing over the large wing, referring to the pattern. Glue the wings to the back of the dress. Glue the pearl head onto the wood ring. Glue the flowers and leaves in place. Glue the pearls to the center of the flowers. Let the glue dry.

HEAVENLY ANGEL
PLACEMENT DIAGRAM

1 SQUARE = 1 INCH

Tiny Trees

Tabletop trees are more than welcome to add holiday sparkle to small areas.

WHAT YOU NEED

Baby's breath, eucalyptus, rose hips, dried hydrangea, and pepper berries
Ribbon; cranberries; needle; waxed dental floss
Miniature baskets; pinecones; thick white crafts glue

HERE'S HOW

1 Glue flowers in baskets and on the top of pinecones. Glue or tie on short lengths of ribbon for hangers. Let dry.

2 For the garland, thread a needle with a 36-inch length of dental floss. Knot one end. String cranberries on the dental floss and knot the opposite end. For longer garlands, leave long tails and tie the ends together. Trim the floss ends.

Fruited Trees

Less expensive than full-size versions, small holiday trees are wonderful backdrops for fruit-slice ornaments.

WHAT YOU NEED

Oranges and lemons
Knife
Ornament hooks
Rose hips

HERE'S HOW

1 Cut ¼-inch-thick slices of oranges and lemons. Place on a paper-towel-covered plate and let dry overnight.

2 For each slice of fruit, poke an ornament hook under the rind. Hang the ornaments on the tree. Tuck sprigs of rose hips between the ornaments.

Jeweled Candlelight

WHAT YOU NEED

Newspapers
Glass spray paint in red and yellow
Glass candle cylinder in proportion to the pedestal
Braid trim
Scissors
Thick white crafts glue
Heavy cake pedestal
Jewelry: earrings, strands of beads, brooches
Hot glue gun; hot-glue sticks
Gems
Glitter paint

Sparkling flea-market jewelry finds a bright new home surrounding a glass candleholder.

HERE'S HOW

1 In a well-ventilated work area, cover work surface with newspapers. Spray a light coat of yellow glass paint on the bottom exterior of the glass cylinder. Spray a light coat of red on the bottom of the cylinder, overlapping colors. Repeat, spraying on two to three light coats of paint, allowing to dry between coats.

2 Cut braid trim to fit top of cylinder. Use crafts glue to secure in place.

3 Place glass cylinder on pedestal. Arrange jewels, starting with largest strands of beads, draping around glass cylinder and beyond edges of pedestal. Hot-glue in place. Hot-glue jewelry around pedestal and base of the glass cylinder. Fill in with small jewelry pieces.

4 To add small gems, place a generous dab of glitter paint onto surface and press gems into paint. Let dry.

Patriotic Pretties

Make these all-American Christmas ball ornaments to celebrate your patriotic spirit. With just a handful of supplies, you can add the sparkle and pizzazz of red, white, and blue to your holiday tree.

WHAT YOU NEED FOR THE REINFORCEMENT ORNAMENT

Matte-finish silver ornament
Hole-punch reinforcement stickers
Liner brush; bowl; fine white glitter
Thick white crafts glue; silver seed beads
Toothpick; fine wire or string

HERE'S HOW

1 Apply stickers to the ornament, leaving space around each sticker. Press gently to adhere edges to the surface.

2 Dilute crafts glue with water. Use a liner brush to apply a coat of diluted glue to the stickers. While the glue is wet, hold the ornament over a bowl and sprinkle glitter over glue, working from top to bottom.

3 To add beads, use a toothpick to apply a dot of glue to the center of each reinforcement; press a silver bead into the adhesive. Hang with fine wire or string to dry.

WHAT YOU NEED FOR THE OTHER ORNAMENTS

Matte ornament; fine- and wide-tip silver paint pens
Thick white crafts glue; fine-liner and flat paintbrushes
Bowl; white glitter; fine wire or string

HERE'S HOW

1 Use fine-tip silver paint pen to outline a design or write words on the ornament. Use a wide-tip paint pen to fill in large areas.

2 For glittered areas, dilute crafts glue with water. Use a liner brush to apply a coat of diluted glue to the painted areas. While the glue is wet, hold the ornament over a bowl and sprinkle glitter over glue, working from top to bottom. Hang with fine wire or string to dry.

Brocade Bell

Rich brocade fabric creates a lovely background for this bell-shape ornament. Braid, ribbon, cord, and circular trims lend elegant appeals.

WHAT YOU NEED

Tracing paper; pencil; scissors
Mat board
Fleece
Thick white crafts glue
12-inch square of brocade fabric
6-inch square of contrasting fabric
Gold cord
¾ yard of ½-inch-wide flat braid
Assorted trims
18 inches of ribbon

BELL PATTERN

HERE'S HOW

1 Trace the pattern, *opposite*. Cut out shape. Trace around shape on mat board and cut out. Glue two layers of fleece on shape, trimming flush with cardboard edge.

2 Line brocade fabric with fleece. Pin a paper pattern to the right side of the fabric. Machine-stitch around the edge. Trim away fleece allowance. Cut out ornament ¾ inch beyond design.

3 Top-stitch a contrasting band of silk fabric horizontally on the bell. Center fabric over mat board and glue excess to back side, clipping as necessary at curves.

4 Glue braid around shape. Glue trims to horizontal band. Let the glue dry. Stitch a cord hanging loop and ribbon bow to the top of the ornament.

Ruffled Wreath

Your tree can glisten with gold. Let the entire family join in the fun of making pretty little ribbon wreaths in assembly-line fashion.

WHAT YOU NEED

6½ yards of 1¼-inch-wide gold-edge organdy ribbon
Scissors
Matching thread
6 inches of gold cord
2½-inch-diameter gold crafts ring with split opening

HERE'S HOW

1 Cut ribbon into two 3-yard lengths. Set aside excess. Lay one ribbon on top of the other, offsetting slightly. Sew a channel down the center by machine- or hand-stitching two parallel lines ¼ inch apart.

2 Open out the ring slightly. Slide the ring down the channel of the ribbon, gathering the ribbon tightly. Press the ends of the ring closed.

3 Tie the remaining ribbon into a bow and tack to the wreath. Tie a cord hanger to the top.

Swirl Ornament

No patterns are necessary for this freehand-design ornament. Simply draw designs, such as stars and spirals, to blanket a frosted globe with silver and gold.

WHAT YOU NEED

Medium-tip metallic marking pens in silver and gold
Frosted clear ball ornament
Fine-tip metallic marking pen in gold
¼-inch-wide gold ribbon

HERE'S HOW

1 Using a silver pen, randomly draw ½-inch star shapes on the ornament. Let dry.

2 Draw slightly smaller gold stars within the silver stars. Fill in with gold. Let dry. Using a fine-tip gold pen, draw small spirals between the stars. Let dry.

3 Thread ribbon through the metal ornament hanger. Tie the ribbon ends into a bow for the hanger.

$\mathscr{M}$istletoe $\mathscr{M}$agic

Kissing Chairs

Spread the wonder of the season with this charming kissing-ball set.

WHAT YOU NEED

Chairs
Screwdriver
Fine sandpaper
Tack cloth
Newspapers
White spray primer
**Acrylic paints in red-orange, pale
    peach, soft yellow, blue-green, pale
    blue-green, white, pale yellow, green,
    turquoise, pale green, lavender, pale
    magenta, orange, pale baby blue,
    peach, pink, yellow, and mauve**
Painting sponge
Medium flat paintbrush
Fine-liner paintbrush
Small flat paintbrush
Tracing paper
Pencil
Scissors
Gold paint pen

HERE'S HOW

1 Remove the seats from the chairs with
   a screwdriver if they are removable.
   Sand rough edges of chair if needed.
   Wipe off dust with a tack cloth.

2 In a well-ventilated work area, cover
   work surface with newspapers. Spray
   white primer onto chair. Let dry. Spray
   a second coat and let dry.

*Mistletoe Magic instructions are continued
on page 227.*

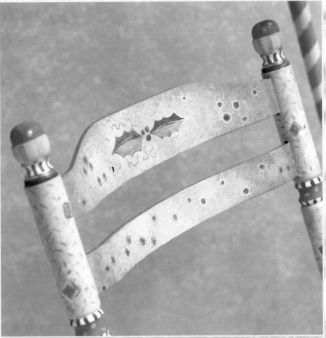

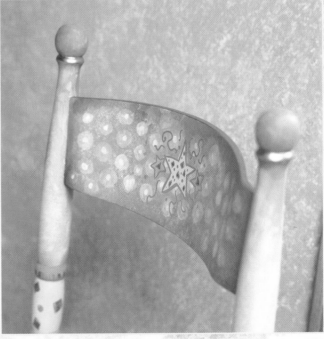

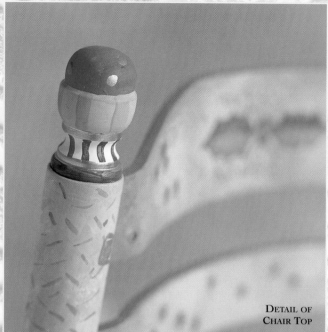

DETAIL OF
CHAIR TOP

DETAIL OF
CHAIR RUNG

DETAIL OF
CHAIR LEG

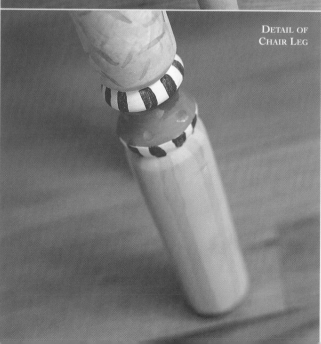

HOLLY CHAIR
BACK PATTERN

STAR CHAIR
BACK PATTERN

3 Using the photos, *pages 224* and *225*, as guides, paint the background areas first. Paint colors with a medium flat brush and blend using a damp sponge. Blend the red-orange into the peach while wet; blend the orange toward the edges. On the chair with stars, blend the turquoise into the pale soft green. On the holly chair sponge white into the soft green areas as shown in Photo 1, *below*. Blend lavender and pale magenta using a sponge, painting lavender around the edges.

4 Trace the holly and star patterns. Cut out and trace onto painted background as shown in Photo 2. Paint in shapes. Paint stripes, dots, and squares using a small flat brush. Thin the white paint to transparent consistency and paint in soft white circles over painted lavender and magenta background. Let dry. Paint white dot in center. Use fine-liner brush to paint short lines on green. Outline shapes and edges with a gold paint pen. Paint the seat, let dry, and reattach to the chair.

Mistletoe Magic instructions are continued on page 228.

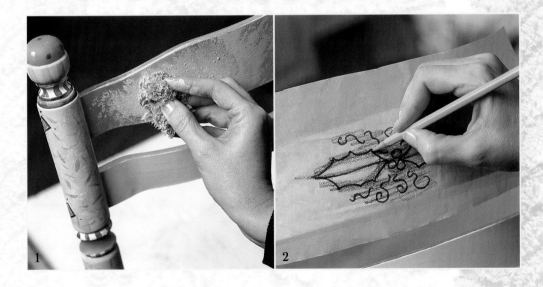

Mistletoe Lamp

WHAT YOU NEED

Acrylic paint in the colors listed for the chairs, *page 225*
**Inexpensive floor lamp, available at thrift shops and
    flea markets**
White 1-inch-wide tape
Medium flat paintbrush; gold paint pen
**6-inch plastic-foam ball, such as
    Styrofoam**
2-inch-wide wire-edge gold ribbon
Hot-glue gun; hot-glue sticks
Straight pins; silk mistletoe

HERE'S HOW

1 For the mistletoe hanger,
paint the lamp pole using
white and pale baby blue;
blend together, painting blue
on top and bottom, with white area
in the middle as shown in Photo 1, *top left*. Let dry.

2 Wind tape around the pole, winding at an even angle all
the length of the pole as shown in Photo 2. Paint the
uncovered portion using pale magenta and peach,
blending with a brush. Paint magenta on top and bottom,
with peach in the middle as shown in Photo 3. Let dry.
Remove the tape. Paint the remainder of the unpainted
areas using the techniques as for the chairs, *page 227.*
Outline areas with gold paint pen. Let dry.

3 Pin a wide wired gold ribbon to the plastic-foam ball.
Wind, twist, and overlap the gold ribbon around the ball
to cover completely as shown in Photo 4. Use straight
pins to hold it in place.

4 If the artificial mistletoe is not an appropriate color, paint
the leaves pale green and the berries peach and mauve,
slightly overlapping the colors. Let dry.

5 Use hot glue and straight pins to adhere mistletoe to
ball. Use pins to attach a gold ribbon to the ball.
Wind the ribbon around the lamp stand and tie
to the end.

DETAIL OF
KISSING BALL

DETAIL OF
LAMP BASE

Jing-a-Ling Stocking

Make this snappy Christmas stocking for your holiday scene. Soft colors are great companions to traditional Christmas reds and greens.

WHAT YOU NEED

Fabric marking pen; ruler; graph paper for pattern
Scissors; pins
⅝ yard of coral moire taffeta (front, back, hanging loop)
½ yard of coordinating stripe fabric (cuff, piping)
⅝ yard of lining fabric
13×20-inch piece of fleece
Matching rayon embroidery floss, decorative-twist rayon thread, and sewing thread
13×20-inch piece of fusible interfacing
2½ yards of ⅛-inch-diameter piping cord
Nine ⅜-inch-diameter gold bells

HERE'S HOW

1 Enlarge the stocking pattern, *page 233*, onto graph paper; cut out.

2 **QUILT THE FABRIC:** For stocking front, cut one 13×20-inch piece from moire taffeta; set aside remaining fabric. Trace the stocking shape onto the right side of fabric; do not cut out shape at this time. Use fabric marking pen and ruler to draw a 1-inch diamond grid covering entire stocking shape. Place the stocking fabric on fleece with the grid up; pin in place outside of the drawn shape.

3 Cut pieces of rayon embroidery floss long enough to cover the grid lines. Separate the floss strands and use three strands of floss along each grid line. To machine-quilt fabric, sew over floss with a narrow zigzag stitch, using decorative-twist rayon thread in needle. Cut out stocking front on traced lines.

4 **SEWING THE STOCKING:** Sew pieces with right sides together, using ½-inch seam allowances, unless otherwise noted.

Jing-a-Ling Stocking instructions are continued on page 232.

Zing-a-Ling Stocking

5 From remaining moire, cut one stocking reversed and one 2×7-inch hanging loop. From stripe fabric, cut one 12×16-inch cuff piece and enough 1½-inch-wide strips to measure 1½ yards in length for piping. From lining fabric, cut two stockings. From interfacing, cut one stocking.

6 Sew together the piping strips to make one long piece. Center the piping cord on wrong side of strip; fold fabric over cord, matching long edges. Use a zipper foot to sew through both fabric layers close to cord. Pin piping to sides and foot of stocking front with raw edges facing out. With zipper foot, sew piping to stocking; clip seam allowance of piping at curves to fit. Trim off excess piping.

7 Align stocking interfacing on wrong side of stocking back; fuse following manufacturer's instructions. Sew stocking back to front along piping stitching line with a zipper foot, leaving top open. Trim seams; clip curves; turn right side out.

8 For cuff, sew the 12-inch edges together, forming a tube. Fold cuff in half lengthwise with wrong sides together, matching raw edges and seams; press. Position remaining piping cord inside the cuff and against the fold; trim excess cord. Sew next to cord with zipper foot. Slip cuff onto stocking with cuff seam at center back with raw edges even; baste.

9 For hanging loop, press under ½ inch on both long edges of 2×7-inch moire piece. Fold in half lengthwise, bringing folded edges together and enclosing the raw edges; press; edge-stitch. Fold strip in half; sew to the top right corner of stocking with raw edges even.

10 Sew lining pieces together, leaving top open and a 4-inch opening in one side for turning. Trim seams; clip curves. Slip stocking into lining, right sides together and seams matching; sew around top of stocking. Pull moire stocking through opening in lining; slip-stitch opening closed. Tuck lining into stocking. Pull cuff away from stocking; sew ¼ inch from top of stocking, through stocking and lining layers. Fold cuff down over stocking. Sew evenly spaced bells along bottom front edge of cuff.

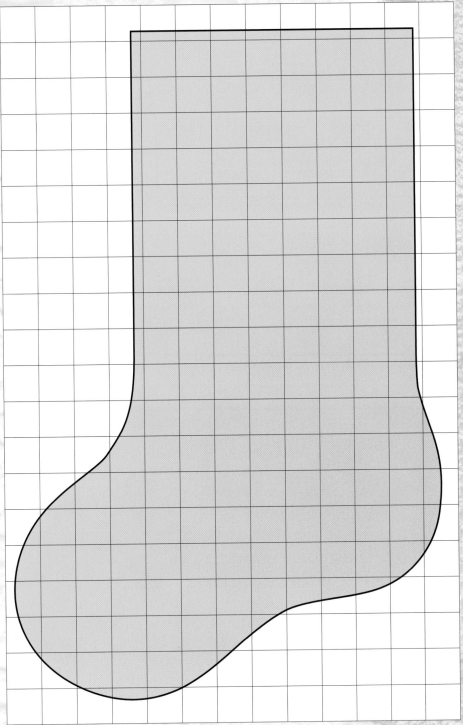

JING-A-LING STOCKING PATTERN   1 SQUARE = 1 INCH

Holiday Mantels

Frosted Forest

WHAT YOU NEED

Miniature snow-flecked trees in bases
1½-inch-wide ribbon
Scissors
Pearls on a string

HERE'S HOW

1 Tie generous ribbon bows at the top of each tree. Trim ribbon ends. Arrange on mantel with pearls.

Pinecone Bottles

WHAT YOU NEED

Small colored bottles
Colored raffia
Scissors
Pinecones

HERE'S HOW

1 Tie raffia bows around bottle necks. Trim ends. Place a pinecone in the top of each bottle. Arrange on mantel.

Topper Finale

WHAT YOU NEED

Glass tree toppers
Tacky wax
Holiday greenery

HERE'S HOW

1 Arrange tree toppers on mantel, securing if necessary with tacky wax. Tuck holiday greenery in arrangement.

Collections make stunning mantel decorations. Group glass finials, miniature snow-kissed trees, and colorful bottles for grand presentations.

$\mathcal{P}$oinsettia $\mathcal{A}$fghan

It may be nippy outside, but you'll keep toasty warm with this lovely wool throw. Several colors of imitation suede create a soft scattering of leaves and poinsettias. A hand-crocheted edge makes a lovely scalloped border.

CROCHET ABBREVIATIONS

Dc = double crochet
Hdc = half double crochet
Rep = repeat
Sc = single crochet
Trc = triple crochet

WHAT YOU NEED

Scissors

1¾ yard of 60-inch-wide, rose-colored boiled wool fabric

Lightweight fusible webbing; straight pins

Six pieces of 9-inch-square imitation suede in four different colors, ranging from pink to burgundy

4×18-inch pieces of five different shades of green imitation suede; thread for bobbin; size H crochet hook

Madeira Glamour metallic overlock thread, colors #12458 (green), #2415 (red), #2465 (turquoise)

Madeira Heavy Metal metallic embroidery thread, #6082 (gold); stabilizing paper for machine embroidery

Twenty-one 8mm gold beads

One 1¾-ounce skein Nature Spun Sport Weight yarn, color N81 (Cranberry Fog) from Brown Sheep Co.

Three 1¾-ounce skeins of Handpaint Originals yarn, color HP40 (Strawberry Patch)

HERE'S HOW

1 Cut wool to a 58-inch square. Enlarge and trace all pattern pieces, *page 238*, onto fusible webbing according to the manufacturer's directions. Trace patterns for three poinsettias, nine assorted leaves, and 10 ivy leaves.

2 Fuse the fusible webbing to wrong side of the imitation suede using a press cloth; cut out. Remove paper backing. Arrange and pin pieces onto wool according to the diagram, *page 239*. With gold thread in top of machine and with a zigzag stitch, machine-appliqué the leaf details and flowers by crouching over glamour thread. Sew seven gold beads to flower centers. Using sport weight yarn, work blanket stitches around edge.

3 For crocheted edging with Handpaint Originals yarn and size H hook work: *Sc in one buttonhole stitch, hdc in next buttonhole stitch, 2 dc in next buttonhole stitch, 3 trc in next buttonhole stitch, 2 dc in next buttonhole stitch, hdc in next buttonhole stitch. Rep from * around outside edge add 2 extra trc at corners. End by slip-stitching to beginning. Secure end of yarn.

POINSETTIA AFGHAN PATTERNS

POINSETTIA AFGHAN ASSEMBLY DIAGRAM

Trapunto Pillows

Trapunto Tree Pillow

WHAT YOU NEED

Graph paper for pattern; scissors
1 yard of 54-inch-wide green fabric
18-inch square of white cotton batiste
Fabric marking pen
Matching sewing thread and decorative-twist
  rayon thread
Knitting needle
Cotton stuffing; straight pins
2 yards of ½-inch-diameter piping cord
18-inch pillow form

HERE'S HOW

1 Note: Measurements for pieces include ½-inch seam allowances. All sewing is done with right sides together, unless otherwise noted. Enlarge and trace the pattern, *page 243.*

2 From green fabric, cut two 18-inch squares and enough 1½-inch-wide bias strips to make 2 yards of piping.

3 Place batiste over enlarged tree pattern; use fabric marking pen to trace tree shape twice, positioning trees as desired and away from the seam allowances. Baste batiste to pillow front with wrong sides together. Using rayon thread in bobbin and a short stitch length, machine-sew over traced lines.

4 To add dimension, stuff the tree shapes between the fabric layers and inside the stitching lines. Cut a small slit in the batiste fabric in between stitching lines and use a knitting needle to poke stuffing between the batiste and pillow front. Hand-sew slit closed with loose stitches.

5 Sew together the piping strips to make one long piece. Center the piping cord on wrong side of strip; fold fabric over cord, matching long edges. Use a zipper foot to sew through both fabric layers close to cord.

The raised star and tree designs on the green and red pillows are made with a sewing method called trapunto. The gold star-shape pillow requires only one pattern piece, which is repeated five times. Gold piping and a star-shape button provide the finishing touches.

Trapunto Pillows instructions continue on pages 242-245.

6 Pin piping to right side of pillow front with raw edges facing out and ends overlapping at center bottom. With zipper foot, sew piping to pillow front; clip seam allowance of piping at corners to fit. Trim off excess piping.

7 Pin pillow back to pillow front with piping sandwiched in between. Sew over previous stitching, rounding corners and leaving a large opening on one side to insert pillow form. Clip corners; turn right side out. Insert pillow form; turn in raw edges, and slip-stitch opening closed.

Trapunto Star Pillow

WHAT YOU NEED

1 yard of 54-inch-wide red fabric
½ yard of white cotton batiste
Matching sewing thread and decorative-twist rayon thread
Cotton stuffing; knitting needle
Tapestry needle
Worsted-weight synthetic yarn; straight pins
2¾ yards of ⅛-inch-diameter piping cord
6×14-inch bolster pillow form
2 yards of decorative cord (ties)
Fabric marking pen; graph paper for pattern

HERE'S HOW

1 Note: These instructions can be adapted to make a smaller or larger pillow. Yardages are based on a 6×14-inch bolster pillow form with a circumference of 19 inches.

2 Measure length and circumference of pillow form. For fabric-cutting dimensions, add 1 inch to each measurement to allow for a ½-inch seam allowance on each side.

3 Using these dimensions, cut one piece each from red fabric and batiste for pillow center. From red fabric, cut two pieces the width of the circumference measurement and 20½ inches long for side pieces and enough 1½-inch-wide bias strips to make 2 yards of piping.

Trapunto Pillows instructions are continued on page 244.

TRAPUNTO STAR
PILLOW PATTERNS

4 Trace patterns, *page 243*, and cut out. Place batiste over star patterns; use fabric marking pen to trace stars as desired, positioning away from the seam allowances. Baste batiste to pillow center with wrong sides together. Using rayon thread in bobbin and a short stitch length, machine-sew over traced lines.

5 To add dimension, stuff the stars between the fabric layers and inside the stitching lines. To stuff large areas, cut a small slit in the batiste fabric and use a knitting needle to poke stuffing between the batiste and pillow fabric. Hand-sew slit closed with loose stitches. For small narrow channels, thread tapestry needle with a length of yarn. At outside point of star, insert needle through batiste fabric between the stitching lines. Pull yarn through channel between the fabric layers, exiting at an inside point of star and re-entering at the same point. Work around the star shape. Repeat to fill channel. Trim yarn.

6 Sew together the piping strips to make one long piece. Center the piping cord on wrong side of strip; fold fabric over cord, matching long edges. Use a zipper foot to sew through both fabric layers close to cord; set aside excess piping cord. Cut piping in half.

7 Pin piping to edges that match the circumference of the pillow form on right side of pillow center with raw edges facing out. With zipper foot, sew piping to pillow center; trim off excess piping. Sew together ends without piping, forming a tube. Turn right side out.

8 For side piece, sew the 20½-inch edges together, forming a tube. Fold side piece in half with wrong sides together, matching raw edges and seams; press. Cut the remaining piping cord in half. Position one piece of piping cord inside the side piece and up against the fold; trim excess cord. Sew next to cord with zipper foot. Baste raw edges together. Repeat for second side piece.

9 Pin a side piece to each open end of pillow center, matching seams and keeping raw edges even. Sew over previous stitching; pull side pieces away from pillow center. Insert pillow form. Cut decorative cord in half. Tie around side pieces; knot ends.

Star Pillow

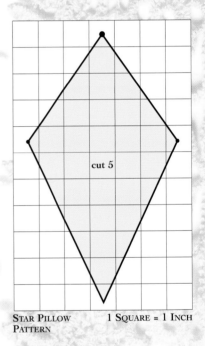

⅝ yard of light gold moire taffeta (piecing, backing);
straight pins

⅓ yard of gold moire taffeta (piecing); scissors

8×12-inch piece of ecru moire taffeta (piecing)

22-inch square of lightweight underlining fabric

Two 12×22-inch pieces of fusible interfacing

Matching sewing thread; 2 yards of ³⁄₁₆-inch-diameter
cord piping with ready-to-sew-in flange; 1-inch-wide
gold star button; polyester fiberfill; template plastic

Here's How

1 All sewing is done with right sides together using ½-inch
seam allowances, unless otherwise noted. Enlarge the
diamond pattern, *below right,* onto template plastic; cut out,
adding ½-inch seam allowances beyond drawn lines.

2 To cut the fabrics, cut the following: from light gold moire,
cut two diamonds and two 12×22-inch backing pieces.
From gold moire, cut two diamonds. From ecru moire,
cut one diamond.

3 Lay out the diamonds, matching dots on pattern. Begin
sewing at small dot and end at large dot; do not sew into
seam allowances. Backstitch at each dot to secure seam.
Trim seam allowances to ¼ inch; press clockwise, flattening
the center seam extensions to form a small star on back.

4 To stabilize bias-cut edges, pin the pieced pillow front to
the underlining fabric with right side up; baste ½ inch from
the raw edges of pillow front, rounding the points. Trim
underlining even with pillow front. Pin piping cord to right
side of pillow front with rounded edge of piping facing
inward and flat extension atop basting line; overlap ends at
center bottom. With zipper foot, sew piping to pillow front;
clip seam allowance of piping at corners. Trim excess piping.

5 Fuse interfacing to backing pieces, following
manufacturer's instructions. Pin and sew long edges of
backing pieces together, leaving a 4-inch-long opening in
the center for turning pillow; press seam allowance open.

6 Pin pillow front to backing fabric, centering pillow front
over the center back seam. Sew over previous stitching,
rounding the points. Clip corners and trim seam
allowances; turn right side out. Stuff pillow firmly with
polyester fiberfill; slip-stitch opening closed. Sew star
button to center of pillow through all layers.

cut 5

Star Pillow Pattern   1 Square = 1 Inch

245

Vintage Postcard Pillow

Share a favorite postcard greeting with family and friends by transferring an enlarged image to white fabric and sewing it to a pillow front.

WHAT YOU NEED

Antique postcard enlarged in color on an 8½×11-inch paper from a photocopy center

11×7-inch piece of white cotton fabric for design transfer

11×7-inch piece of photo transfer paper

Scissors

½ yard of 45-inch-wide red velveteen fabric

Matching thread

#5 green pearl cotton for edging

Metallic green embroidery floss

Three ½-inch buttons

12 assorted ½-inch jingle bells

Pillow form

HERE'S HOW

1 Center the enlarged postcard design on piece of photo transfer paper. Transfer the design onto the white fabric according to the manufacturer's directions.

2 Cut two velveteen horizontal sashing strips, each 3¼×16½ inches. Cut velveteen backing for pillow, allowing for an overlapping buttonhole closure.

3 Using ¼-inch seams, stitch horizontal sashing strips to the top and bottom edge of the white fabric with the transferred design. Stitch the vertical sashing strips to each side of the design.

4 Right sides facing, stitch pillow front to back along outer edges. Trim the corners. Turn to right side. Topstitch ¾ inch from outer edge. Using 1 strand each of green pearl cotton and metallic green floss, work long and short buttonhole stitches around the edge. Sew on buttons for back closure.

5 Sew three jingle bells to each corner of the design. Insert the pillow form.

A MERRY
CHRISTMAS
AND ALL
GOOD WISHES

Just Desserts

"Christmas—that magic blanket that wraps itself about us, that something so intangible that it is like a fragrance. It may weave a spell of nostalgia. Christmas may be a day of feasting, or of prayer, but always it will be a day of remembrance—a day in which we think of everything we have ever loved."

—Augusta E. Rundel

Tempting Tarts

Because guests usually stand at open house parties, easy-to-eat finger desserts are welcome treats — and you can make these a week ahead. Try spicy Mincemeat Tarts sprinkled with sugar and creamy Mini Chess Tarts dotted with jam.

Mincemeat Tarts

WHAT YOU NEED

1½ cups prepared mincemeat
1 teaspoon finely shredded orange peel
2 cups all-purpose flour
⅛ teaspoon salt
6 tablespoons butter
3 tablespoons shortening
4 to 6 tablespoons cold water
Milk
Sugar

HERE'S HOW

1 Preheat oven to 375°F. Grease bottoms and sides of eight 2½-inch tart pans or muffin cups; set aside. For filling, combine mincemeat and orange peel; set aside. In a large mixing bowl stir together flour and salt. Using a pastry blender, cut in butter and shortening until pieces are the size of small peas. Sprinkle 1 tablespoon cold water over part of mixture; gently toss. Push to side. Repeat with remaining water, 1 tablespoon at a time, until all is moistened. Form into a ball.

2 Flatten dough on a lightly floured surface. Roll from center to edges to ⅛-inch thickness. With cutters or the top of a glass, cut eight 4-inch rounds and eight 3-inch rounds. Fit larger rounds into tart pans or muffin cups. Spoon about 3 tablespoons filling into each pastry-lined pan, filling almost to top. Moisten edges with water. Fit smaller rounds over filling. Seal and flute edges. Prick tops. Brush with milk and sprinkle with sugar. If using tart pans, place on a baking sheet. Bake in the preheated oven for 30 minutes or until browned. Cool in pans on a wire rack. Remove from pans. If desired, cover and freeze for up to 1 week. Thaw. Makes 8 tarts.

Mini Chess Tarts

WHAT YOU NEED

- 1/2 of 11-ounce package
  piecrust mix
  (1 1/4 cups)
- 1/4 cup plain yogurt
- 1 slightly beaten egg
- 1/3 cup sugar
- 2 tablespoons butter,
  melted
- 1 tablespoon milk
- 1 teaspoon cornmeal
- 1/4 teaspoon finely
  shredded lemon peel
- 1 teaspoon lemon juice
  Red and/or green jelly

HERE'S HOW

1 Preheat oven to 350°F.
In a medium mixing bowl combine piecrust mix and
yogurt; stir until moistened. Divide into 18 pieces. Form
into balls. Press into bottom and up sides of 18 ungreased
1 3/4-inch muffin cups.

2 In a small mixing bowl stir together egg, sugar, butter,
milk, cornmeal, lemon peel, and lemon juice. Spoon about
2 teaspoons filling into each pastry-lined cup. Bake in the
preheated oven for 25 to 30 minutes or until filling is
golden and set. Cool on a wire rack. If desired, cover and
freeze for up to 1 week. Thaw. To serve, spoon jelly onto
centers of tarts. Makes 18 tarts.

Lemon Curd Pastry

Lemon Curd Pastry is quick, light, and good-tasting with any fruit. The tangy-sweet lemon curd spread lies under the berries and gives them a tart kick; if you prefer a mellower flavor, try lemon pudding.

WHAT YOU NEED

½ of 17¼-ounce package frozen puff pastry (1 sheet), thawed
1 slightly beaten egg white
1 teaspoon water
Coarse sugar or granulated sugar
⅔ cup lemon curd (room temperature)*
⅔ cup dairy sour cream
¼ teaspoon ground ginger
1 to 2 drops almond extract
3 cups desired fresh berries, such as blackberries, raspberries, blueberries, and/or quartered strawberries
¼ cup sliced almonds, toasted
2 tablespoons honey
Powdered sugar, optional

HERE'S HOW

1 Preheat oven to 375°F. On a lightly floured surface, unfold pastry and roll into a 15×10-inch rectangle. From edges of rectangle cut 2 lengthwise ¾-inch-wide strips and 2 crosswise ¾-inch-wide strips. Set aside. Place pastry rectangle on ungreased baking sheet. Combine egg white and water; brush onto rectangle. Place pastry strips on edges of rectangle; trim to fit. Brush strips with egg-white mixture; sprinkle with coarse sugar. Prick bottom of pastry several times with fork. Bake in preheated oven for 20 to 25 minutes or until light brown. Cool on a wire rack.

2 In a medium mixing bowl stir lemon curd until smooth. Stir together sour cream, ginger, and almond extract; fold into curd. Spread on cooled pastry. Cover and chill until serving time, up to 4 hours. Before serving, top with berries and sliced almonds. Drizzle with honey. Sprinkle with powdered sugar, if desired. Makes 8 servings.

Lemon curd is a tangy-sweet English spread. Look for it in the jam or specialty foods section of a supermarket or gourmet food shop.

Chocolate Torte

This Chocolate Torte, filled with walnuts and chocolate pieces and smothered in a chocolate glaze, may be the first dessert to disappear. If you serve wine, provide a Cabernet Sauvignon, which always marries well with chocolate.

WHAT YOU NEED

1½ cups walnuts or pecans
¾ cup granulated sugar
¼ cup cocoa
¼ cup semisweet chocolate pieces
1 teaspoon baking powder
¼ teaspoon baking soda
5 eggs
1 teaspoon vanilla
   Chocolate Glaze
   Chocolate Curls; powdered sugar

HERE'S HOW

1 Preheat oven to 350°F. In a food processor bowl combine nuts, sugar, cocoa, chocolate pieces, baking powder, and soda. Process until nuts are ground. Add eggs and vanilla; process until nearly smooth. Spread mixture evenly in a greased and floured 9-inch round cake pan. Bake in the preheated oven for 35 minutes.

2 Cool for 10 minutes. Remove from pan; place on a serving plate. Cool completely. Spread with Chocolate Glaze. Top with Chocolate Curls; dust with powdered sugar. Chill until serving time. Makes 8 to 10 servings.

3 CHOCOLATE GLAZE: In a small saucepan melt 3 ounces (3 squares) semisweet chocolate and 3 tablespoons butter over low heat, stirring constantly. Remove from heat; stir in 1½ cups sifted powdered sugar and 2 tablespoons hot water. Add more hot water if needed to make pouring consistency.

4 CHOCOLATE CURLS: Carefully draw a vegetable peeler across the broad surface of two or three 2-ounce chocolate baking bars at room temperature. Use immediately or carefully place on paper towels in a single layer in a covered storage container. Store at room temperature or chill.

Cheesecake & Berries

WHAT YOU NEED

1½ cups finely crushed
  chocolate sandwich
  cookies
3 tablespoons butter,
  melted
3 8-ounce packages
  cream cheese
½ cup sugar
2 tablespoons all-purpose
  flour
1 teaspoon vanilla
2 egg whites
1 cup whipping cream
1 12-ounce package
  unsweetened red
  raspberries, thawed
½ cup sugar
1 teaspoon lemon juice

HERE'S HOW

1 Preheat oven to 375°F. For crust, combine cookie crumbs
  and melted butter. Press into bottom of greased 8- or 9-
  inch springform pan. In a large mixing bowl combine
  cream cheese, ½ cup sugar, flour, and vanilla. Beat with
  electric mixer on medium speed until fluffy. Add egg
  whites, beating on low speed just until combined. Stir in
  whipping cream. Pour into crust-lined pan.

2 Place pan in a shallow baking pan in oven. Bake in the
  preheated oven 40 to 45 minutes for 8-inch pan or 30 to
  35 minutes for 9-inch pan or until center appears nearly
  set when lightly shaken. Cool 15 minutes. Loosen crust
  from pan sides. Cool 30 minutes more; remove sides of
  pan. Cool completely. Chill at least 4 hours.

3 Blend raspberries in a blender container just until smooth.
  Press through sieve. Combine raspberries, ½ cup sugar,
  and lemon juice in saucepan. Heat just until sugar
  dissolves; cool. Cover and chill. Serve cheesecake with
  sauce. Makes 12 servings.

This mouthwatering cheesecake covers a crushed chocolate cookie crust. The sauce of berries, lemon juice, and sugar takes only minutes to make.

255

Royal Christmas Cake

Bursting with candied fruits and almonds and an almond-paste filling, Royal Christmas Cake is a feast for the senses. This international favorite comes from England. It is aged two weeks before serving, and during that two weeks, it is kept moist and flavorful with rum, brandy, or orange juice.

2	cups all-purpose flour
1	teaspoon ground cinnamon
½	teaspoon baking powder
¼	teaspoon baking soda
¼	teaspoon ground nutmeg
¼	teaspoon ground cloves
1½	cups currants
1½	cups dark or light raisins
1½	cups diced mixed candied fruits and peels
1	cup candied red and/or green cherries
1	cup ground almonds (2 ounces)
4	eggs
1	cup sugar
¾	cup margarine or butter, melted
½	cup rum, brandy, or orange juice
3	tablespoons lemon juice
	Rum, brandy, or orange juice
1	8-ounce can almond paste
	Royal Icing
	Fresh bay leaves (optional)

HERE'S HOW

1 Preheat oven to 300°F. Grease two 9×1½-inch round baking pans. Line bottom and sides with parchment or waxed paper; grease paper. Set aside.

2 Stir flour, cinnamon, baking powder, baking soda, nutmeg, and cloves together in a large mixing bowl. Stir in currants, raisins, candied fruits and peels, cherries, and almonds. Set aside.

3 Beat eggs slightly with a fork. Stir eggs; sugar; margarine; the ½ cup rum, brandy, or orange juice; and lemon juice together in a mixing bowl until combined. Stir into flour mixture; pour into prepared pans.

4 Bake in the preheated oven for 1¼ to 1½ hours or until a toothpick inserted near the center comes out clean. (Cover pans loosely with foil after 1 hour of baking to prevent overbrowning.) Cool in pans on a wire rack.

5 Remove cooled cake from pans. Moisten 100-percent-cotton cheesecloth with additional rum, brandy, or orange juice. Wrap cake layers separately in cheesecloth. Wrap with foil. Refrigerate for 1 to 2 weeks. Remoisten cheesecloth with rum, brandy, or orange juice every 3 days or when dry.

6 To assemble, unwrap cake layers. Place one cake layer, top side down, on a serving plate. Spread with half of the almond paste. (If paste is too thick to spread, divide it in half; form each half into a ball. Place each ball between two sheets of waxed paper; flatten slightly with a rolling pin and roll each portion from center to edges to 10 inches in diameter. Remove one sheet of paper from one circle; trim to form a 9-inch circle. Invert onto cake. Peel off remaining paper.)

7 Spread some Royal Icing over almond paste on first cake layer. Add second cake layer, top side up; top with remaining paste. Frost top and sides of cake with remaining Royal Icing. Garnish with bay leaves, if desired. Makes 16 servings.

8 ROYAL ICING: Beat 4 cups sifted powdered sugar, ½ cup water, ¼ cup meringue powder, and 1 teaspoon vanilla with an electric mixer on high speed for 7 to 10 minutes or until very stiff. Use immediately; cover icing in bowl with a damp paper towel while you work. Makes 3½ cups.

9 TO MAKE AHEAD: Refrigerate frosted cake, covered, up to 1 week; or freeze cake up to 6 weeks.

Della Robbia Fruit Tart

Lovely to look at and delicious to eat, Della Robbia Fruit Tart is a fragrant blend of fresh and dried fruit and pecans, covered with an artistically painted pastry crust.

WHAT YOU NEED

Rich Tart Pastry
3 medium apples or pears (about 1 pound)
¼ cup sugar
1 tablespoon all-purpose flour
¼ teaspoon ground nutmeg
¼ cup chopped pecans
¼ cup dried cherries or raisins
Pastry Paint

HERE'S HOW

1 Divide Rich Tart Pastry dough in half. For bottom pastry, roll one-half of dough on a lightly floured surface to an 11-inch circle. Trim to 10-inch circle, reserving dough scraps. Transfer pastry circle to baking sheet; set aside.

2 Peel apples or pears; cut fruit in half lengthwise and core. With cut sides down, cut each fruit half into eight lengthwise slices. Do not separate slices. Set aside.

3 Stir sugar, flour, and nutmeg together. Sprinkle about half of the sugar mixture over pastry circle on baking sheet. Sprinkle with pecans and cherries or raisins. Arrange fruit halves, cut sides down, in a circle on pastry about 1 inch from the edge. Press down on fruit halves to slightly fan out slices. Sprinkle with remaining sugar mixture.

4 For top pastry, roll remaining dough into a 12½-inch circle. Trim to 11½-inch circle; reserve scraps. Place pastry on fruit, draping over fruit and matching edges of pastry circles. Press pastry around fruit, being careful not to stretch pastry. Fold edges of top pastry under bottom pastry. Seal and crimp edge. Cut a 1½-inch hole in center to form a ring; crimp pastry at center.

5 Preheat oven to 375°. Roll dough scraps to ⅛ inch thick. Using a knife or small cookie cutters, cut fruit and leaf shapes from the dough. Lightly brush underside of cutouts with water; press cutouts onto top pastry. Brush tops of cutouts with Pastry Paint as desired.

6 Bake in the preheated oven 30 to 40 minutes or until golden. (Cover with foil after 20 minutes, if necessary,

to prevent overbrowning.) Cool on baking sheet for
10 minutes. Carefully transfer tart to serving plate.
Serve warm. Makes 6 servings.

7 **RICH TART PASTRY:** Place 1 cup cold butter and 2½ cups
all-purpose flour in a mixing bowl; cut with pastry blender
until pieces are the size of small peas. Stir together
2 beaten egg yolks and 2 tablespoons ice water in a small
bowl. Gradually stir egg yolk mixture into flour mixture.
Add 2 to 4 tablespoons additional water, 1 tablespoon at a
time, until all dough is moistened. Gently knead dough just
until a ball forms. Before rolling, cover dough with plastic
wrap and chill in the refrigerator for 30 to 60 minutes or
until dough is easy to handle, if necessary.

8 **PASTRY PAINT:** Stir together 2 slightly beaten egg yolks
and 2 teaspoons water in a small bowl. Divide mixture
among three or four custard cups. Stir a few drops of
food coloring into each cup. Brush onto pastry cutouts
before baking.

Steamed Ginger Pudding

Steaming makes these cakelike puddings moist and tender.

WHAT YOU NEED

- ⅓ cup sugar
- 1 egg
- ⅓ cup butter or margarine, melted
- 2 cups all-purpose flour
- 1 teaspoon ground ginger
- 1 teaspoon ground cinnamon
- ¾ teaspoon baking soda
- ¼ teaspoon salt
- ¾ cup hot water
- ⅓ cup molasses
- 3 tablespoons honey
- Brandy Cream Sauce
- Shredded orange peel (optional)

HERE'S HOW

1 Preheat oven to 350°F. Beat sugar and egg in a mixing bowl with an electric mixer on medium to high speed for 4 minutes or until fluffy. Add butter and beat well.

2 Stir together flour, ginger, cinnamon, baking soda, and ¼ teaspoon salt in another mixing bowl. Combine hot water, molasses, and honey in a small mixing bowl. Alternately add flour mixture and water mixture to egg mixture, beating after each addition until just combined.

3 Lightly grease eight 6-ounce custard cups; fill ⅔ full with batter. Cover each cup tightly with lightly greased foil. Place in a baking pan on an oven rack. Pour boiling water in the baking pan around the cups until water is about halfway up the outside of the cups.

4 Bake in preheated oven about 45 minutes or until the pudding springs back when touched, adding more boiling water to the pan, if necessary. Let cool in cups on a wire rack for 5 minutes. Unmold puddings; cool 15 to 20 minutes. Serve warm with Brandy Cream Sauce. Top with shredded orange peel, if desired. Makes 8 servings.

5 **BRANDY CREAM SAUCE:** Beat ¾ cup whipping cream and ¼ cup sifted powdered sugar until soft peaks form. Stir in 1 tablespoon brandy. Cover and chill until serving time.

Mocha Rum Cheesecake

WHAT YOU NEED

1½ cups finely crushed
    oatmeal cookies (12 to
    14 cookies)
¼ cup butter, melted
¼ cup rum
1 tablespoon instant
    coffee crystals
3 8-ounce packages
    cream cheese, softened
1 cup sugar
4 ounces semisweet
    chocolate pieces,
    melted and cooled
2 tablespoons all-purpose
    flour
1 teaspoon vanilla
3 eggs
  Fresh raspberries
  Chocolate Ribbons and Leaves (see page 288)

HERE'S HOW

1 Preheat oven to 375°F. In mixing bowl toss together
cookies and butter. Press firmly onto bottom and
1½ inches up sides of 9-inch springform pan; set aside.

2 Stir together rum and coffee crystals; set aside. In large bowl
beat cream cheese, sugar, chocolate, flour, and vanilla just
until combined. Add eggs. Beat on low speed 30 seconds
or just until combined. Do not overbeat. Stir in rum
mixture. Pour mixture onto crust. Bake in the preheated
oven 35 to 40 minutes or until center appears nearly set
when shaken. Cool on a wire rack 10 minutes. With a
knife or metal spatula, loosen cheesecake from sides of
pan. Cool cheesecake 2 hours on wire rack; cover and
refrigerate 4 hours before serving. (Or freeze, uncovered,
for 1 hour. Remove bottom of pan. Transfer to a large
freezer bag. Seal, label, and freeze for up to 3 months. Thaw
cheesecake, loosely covered, in refrigerator about 24 hours.)

3 To serve, top cheesecake with fresh raspberries. Garnish
with Chocolate Ribbons and Leaves. Serves 12.

*Piled high
with fresh
raspberries,
this cheesecake
bursts with
flavor.
Chocolate
Ribbons and
Leaves
gift-wrap the
delicious mocha
and rum
cheesecake.*

Mixed Fruit Tart

Cream cheese, amaretto, brown sugar, and fruit make this Mixed Fruit Tart truly tempting.

WHAT YOU NEED

½ of 15-ounce package folded, refrigerated, unbaked piecrust (1 crust)

1 8-ounce package cream cheese, softened

1 3-ounce package cream cheese, softened

½ cup amaretto or ¼ cup milk and ¼ teaspoon almond extract

3 tablespoons packed brown sugar

2–3 cups chilled assorted fresh fruit such as sliced plums, kiwi fruit, peaches, and blueberries, halved strawberries, seedless grapes, and/or raspberries

3–4 tablespoons apple jelly, melted

HERE'S HOW

1 Preheat oven to 450°F. Let piecrust stand 20 minutes at room temperature. On a lightly floured surface roll pastry to 11-inch circle. Transfer to 9-inch tart pan with removable bottom. Ease pastry into pan; do not stretch it. Press pastry into fluted sides of tart pan and trim edges. With a fork, prick bottom and sides of pastry. Line pastry shell with double thickness of foil. Bake in the preheated oven for 5 minutes. Remove foil. Bake 7 to 9 minutes more or until pastry is golden brown. Cool pasty shell in pan on wire rack.

2 In bowl beat cream cheese, amaretto, and brown sugar until smooth. Spread mixture over cooled pastry. (You can cover and chill tart up to 4 hours.)

3 Before serving, remove sides of pan and place tart on a serving platter. Top mixture with desired fruits. Drizzle with melted jelly. Makes 8 servings.

Raspberry Truffle Cake

WHAT YOU NEED

- 16 ounces semisweet chocolate, cut up
- ½ cup butter
- 1 tablespoon sugar
- 1½ teaspoons flour
  Raspberry liqueur, optional
- 4 eggs, separated
  Sweetened Whipped Cream
  Fresh raspberries
  Chocolate Curls
- ¾ cup seedless raspberry jam, melted

HERE'S HOW

1 Preheat oven to 350°F. In a heavy saucepan combine chocolate and butter. Cook and stir over low heat until chocolate melts. Remove from heat. Stir in sugar, flour, and 1 teaspoon raspberry liqueur, if desired. With a wooden spoon, beat in yolks, one at a time, just until combined; set aside.

2 In a bowl beat egg whites with an electric mixer on high speed until stiff peaks form. Fold in chocolate mixture. Pour into greased 8-inch springform pan. Bake in the preheated oven 25 minutes or until edges puff. Cool on rack 30 minutes. Remove sides of pan; cool. Chill, covered, 4 to 24 hours.

3 To serve, top with Sweetened Whipped Cream, raspberries, and Chocolate Curls. Drizzle each piece with 1 tablespoon melted jam. Serves 12.

4 SWEETENED WHIPPED CREAM: Chill a mixing bowl and beaters of an electric mixer in refrigerator. In chilled bowl combine 1 cup whipping cream, 2 tablespoons powdered sugar, and ½ teaspoon vanilla. Beat with chilled beaters on medium speed until soft peaks form. Makes 2 cups.

5 CHOCOLATE CURLS: Draw vegetable peeler across bar of chocolate (or white baking bar with cocoa butter). Transfer curls to top of cake with toothpick or wooden skewer.

To make chocolate curls to garnish this Raspberry Truffle Cake, draw a vegetable peeler across a bar of chocolate and carefully transfer the curls to the cake. Pile on as many as you like.

263

Pies Aplenty

Holiday gatherings always
beckon with decadent pies.
The recipes for this tempting
assortment begin on page 266.

Pies Aplenty

For those who love a good fruit pie, this one will soon be on the top of the list.

Holiday Apple-Cranberry Pie

WHAT YOU NEED

   Pastry
2 cups cranberries
¾ cup packed brown sugar
¼ to ½ cup granulated sugar
⅓ cup all-purpose flour
1 teaspoon ground cinnamon
4 cups sliced cooking apples
2 tablespoons butter or margarine
   Milk
   Granulated sugar
   Sugared cranberries* (optional)

HERE'S HOW

1 Prepare Pastry. Divide in half. On lightly floured surface, roll one-half to a 12-inch-diameter circle. Fit into a 9-inch pie plate. Trim pastry ½ inch beyond edge of pie plate. Roll out the remaining pastry to a 12-inch-diameter circle. Cover and set aside.

2 Preheat oven to 375°F. If you like, chop the 2 cups of cranberries. In a large bowl toss together the brown sugar, the ¼ to ½ cup granulated sugar, the flour, and cinnamon. Add apples and cranberries; mix well. Turn fruit mixture into pastry-lined pie plate. Dot with butter.

3 Cut the rolled-out pastry into ½-inch-wide strips. Weave strips over filling to make a lattice. Press ends of strips into rim of crust. Fold bottom pastry over strips. Seal; flute edge. If you like, roll out pastry scraps and cut into decorative shapes. Brush crust with milk. If using, press shapes into crust. Sprinkle crust with some granulated sugar.

4 Cover edge of crust with foil. Bake for 25 minutes. Remove foil; bake for 20 to 25 minutes more or until golden. Cool on wire rack. Makes 8 servings.

5 **PASTRY:** Stir together 2 cups all-purpose flour and ½ teaspoon salt. Cut in ⅔ cup shortening or lard

until the pieces are the size of small peas. Sprinkle 6 to 7 tablespoons water over mixture, 1 tablespoon at a time, tossing with a fork between additions of water and pushing mixture to side of bowl. (Add only enough water to moisten all of the mixture.)

*NOTE: *To make sugared cranberries, dip cranberries in refrigerated egg product, then roll in sugar.*

German Chocolate Pie

WHAT YOU NEED

Pastry Shell
1   4-ounce package German sweet chocolate
¼   cup butter or margarine
1   12-ounce can (1⅔ cups) evaporated milk
1½ cups sugar
3   tablespoons cornstarch
⅛   teaspoon salt
2   slightly beaten eggs
1   teaspoon vanilla
1⅓ cups coconut
½   cup chopped nuts

HERE'S HOW

1 Prepare the Pastry Shell, except don't prick it or bake it.

2 Preheat oven to 375°F. In a heavy small saucepan warm chocolate and butter over low heat until chocolate melts, stirring occasionally. Remove from heat. Stir evaporated milk into the chocolate mixture.

3 In a medium mixing bowl combine sugar, cornstarch, and salt. Stir in the eggs and vanilla.

4 Add the chocolate mixture to the egg mixture, stirring well. Pour into the prepared shell. Combine coconut and nuts. Sprinkle over the filling.

For a change from traditional fruit pies, this chocolaty version will be an appreciated variation.

Pies Aplenty recipes are continued on pages 268–269.

Pies Aplenty

5 Cover edge of crust with foil. Bake in preheated oven for 25 minutes. Remove foil; continue baking for 25 to 30 minutes more or until puffed and browned. (Filling will be soft.) Cool on a wire rack. Chill for at least 4 hours. Makes 8 servings.

6 **PASTRY SHELL:** In a mixing bowl, stir together 1¼ cups all-purpose flour and ¼ teaspoon salt. Cut in ⅓ cup shortening or lard until the pieces are the size of small peas. Sprinkle 3 to 4 tablespoons water over mixture, 1 tablespoon at a time, tossing with a fork between additions of water and pushing mixture to side of bowl. (Add only enough water to moisten all of the mixture.) Form dough into a ball. On a lightly floured surface, roll dough to form a 12-inch diameter circle. Wrap pastry around rolling pin. Unroll onto a 9-inch pie plate. Ease pastry into pie plate, being careful not to stretch pastry. Trim pastry to ½ inch beyond edge of pie plate; fold under extra pastry. Flute edge.

Each layer of this pie offers a heavenly flavor. From the bottom crust to the peaked topping, you'll savor every bite.

Blueberry Custard Pie

WHAT YOU NEED

    Pastry Shell
- ½ cup sugar
- 3 tablespoons cornstarch
- ⅛ teaspoon ground cinnamon
- 3 cups frozen or fresh blueberries
- 3 tablespoons orange juice
- 1¼ cups milk
- 3 egg yolks
- ½ cup sugar
- 2 tablespoons cornstarch
- ⅛ teaspoon salt
- ½ teaspoon lemon extract or lemon juice
- 3 egg whites
- ½ teaspoon cream of tartar
- 6 tablespoons sugar

HERE'S HOW

1 Prepare Pastry Shell, except don't prick it or bake it.

2 In a saucepan mix ½ cup sugar, 3 tablespoons cornstarch, and cinnamon. Stir in the blueberries and orange juice. Cook and stir until mixture is bubbly. Cover; set aside.

3 **For custard:** In a saucepan combine milk, egg yolks, ½ cup sugar, the 2 tablespoons cornstarch, and salt. Cook and stir until bubbly. Cook and stir for 2 minutes more. Stir in lemon extract. Cover and set aside.

4 In a medium mixing bowl beat egg whites and cream of tartar with an electric mixer until soft peaks form (tips curl). Gradually add the 6 tablespoons sugar, beating until stiff peaks form (tips stand straight).

5 Preheat oven to 350°F. Pour berry mixture into Pastry Shell. Carefully spread custard over blueberry mixture. Spread egg white mixture over custard, sealing to edges.

6 Bake in preheated oven for 15 minutes. Cool on a wire rack. Store in the refrigerator. Makes 8 servings.

7 **PASTRY SHELL:** In a mixing bowl, stir together 1¼ cups all-purpose flour and ¼ teaspoon salt. Cut in ⅓ cup shortening or lard until the pieces are the size of small peas. Sprinkle 3 to 4 tablespoons water over mixture, 1 tablespoon at a time, tossing with a fork between additions of water and pushing mixture to side of bowl. (Add only enough water to moisten all of the mixture.) Form dough into a ball. On a lightly floured surface, roll dough to form a 12-inch diameter circle. Wrap pastry around rolling pin. Unroll onto a 9-inch pie plate. Ease pastry into pie plate, being careful not to stretch pastry. Trim pastry to ½ inch beyond edge of pie plate; fold under extra pastry. Flute edge.

Elegant Desserts

The perfect ending to Christmas dinner, these lovely desserts will long be remembered. Turn the page to make Weihnachten Kuchen, Pear-Chocolate Mousse Tart, and Jumbo Apple Dumplings.

Elegant Desserts

This delicious layered dessert will be the perfect sweet ending to a holiday dinner.

Weihnachten Kuchen

WHAT YOU NEED

1½ cups all-purpose flour
 2 teaspoons baking powder
 1 cup sugar
½ cup butter, softened
 4 egg yolks
 1 teaspoon vanilla
½ cup milk
 4 egg whites
 1 teaspoon vanilla
⅛ teaspoon cream of tartar
1½ cups sugar
¼ cup chopped walnuts or pecans
1½ cups whipping cream
   Chopped nuts (optional)

HERE'S HOW

1 Preheat oven to 350°F. Stir together the flour and baking powder. Set aside.

2 In a large bowl beat the 1 cup sugar and the butter with an electric mixer until the mixture is fluffy. Add the egg yolks and 1 teaspoon vanilla and beat the mixture until light.

3 Add the flour mixture and milk alternately to sugar mixture, beating with mixer on low speed just until combined.

4 Turn batter into 2 greased and floured 9×1½-inch round baking pans, spreading it evenly in the pans.

5 **For meringue:** In a clean bowl, beat the egg whites, 1 teaspoon vanilla, and cream of tartar until soft peaks form. Gradually beat in the 1½ cups sugar until stiff peaks form. Spoon mixture over batter in pans; sprinkle with nuts.

6 Bake layers in the preheated oven for about 30 minutes or until done. Let layers cool in pans on wire racks for 10 minutes. Remove layers from pans to wire racks; cool.

7 Whip the cream just to soft peaks (tips curl). Place 1 layer on a serving plate, meringue side up. Spread with some of

the whipped cream. Top the first layer with the second layer, meringue side up. Top with remaining whipped cream. If desired, top with nuts. Makes 12 servings.

Pear-Chocolate Mousse Tart

WHAT YOU NEED

Pastry Shell
⅓ **cup sugar**
2 **tablespoons butter or margarine**
4 **cups coarsely chopped and peeled pears (4 medium)**
1 **tablespoon pear liqueur**
1 **cup whipping cream**
¼ **cup sugar**
2 **slightly beaten eggs**
2 **ounces unsweetened chocolate, chopped**
2 **ounces semisweet chocolate, chopped**
1 **egg yolk**
½ **cup water**
2 **tablespoons sugar**
1 **cup whipping cream**
Fresh raspberries and mint leaves (optional)

HERE'S HOW

1 Prepare Pastry Shell, except don't place it in a pie plate. Preheat oven to 450°F. On lightly floured surface, roll out the pastry to a 12-inch circle. Ease the pastry into a 10-inch tart pan; flute the edge. Cover the edge and line pastry with a double thickness of heavy foil. Bake in preheated oven for 8 minutes. Remove the foil and bake for 4 to 6 minutes more or until the pastry is golden. Cool on a wire rack. Reduce oven heat to 325°F.

2 In a large skillet combine ⅓ cup sugar and the butter. Cook and stir until butter melts. Stir in pears. Cook over medium heat for 12 to 15 minutes or until sugar turns a caramel color; stir occasionally. Remove from heat; stir in liqueur.

Top this tart with piped chocolate mousse and fresh raspberries for a beautiful presentation.

Elegant Desserts recipes are continued on pages 274–275.

Elegant Desserts

3 In a bowl combine 1 cup whipping cream, the ¼ cup sugar and the 2 slightly beaten eggs until mixed. Spread pear mixture in tart. Carefully pour in the cream mixture.

4 Bake in preheated 325°F oven for 25 to 30 minutes or until a knife inserted near the center comes out clean. If the edges brown too quickly, cover with foil. Cool on wire rack.

5 **For mousse:** In heavy saucepan, melt unsweetened chocolate and semisweet chocolate. In another saucepan, mix egg yolk with water and the 2 tablespoons sugar. Cook over medium heat for about 6 minutes or until slightly thickened. Remove from heat. Quickly stir in melted chocolate. Let stand for 25 minutes.

6 Beat 1 cup whipping cream just to soft peaks (tips curl). Fold into mousse mixture. Pipe or spread some of the mousse on top of tart. Serve remaining mousse with tart. If desired, top with raspberries and mint leaves. Store tart in refrigerator. Makes 10 servings.

7 **PASTRY SHELL:** Stir together 2 cups flour and ½ teaspoon salt. Cut in ⅔ cup shortening or lard until the pieces are the size of small peas. Sprinkle 6 to 7 tablespoons water over mixture, 1 tablespoon at a time, tossing with a fork between additions of water and pushing mixture to side of bowl. (Add only enough water to moisten all of the mixture.)

Jumbo Apple Dumplings

WHAT YOU NEED

  2 cups all-purpose flour
  2 teaspoons baking powder
  1 teaspoon salt
  ⅔ cup shortening
  ⅓ to ½ cup milk
  6 medium cooking apples, peeled and cored
    (about 5 ounces each)
  1 cup sugar
  1¼ teaspoons ground cinnamon

      2 tablespoons butter or margarine
   1½ cups sugar
   1½ cups water
      ¼ teaspoon ground cinnamon
      ¼ teaspoon ground nutmeg
      3 tablespoons butter or margarine
         Sugared cranberries* (see page 267) (optional)
         Ice cream or cream

Dinner guests will know the occasion is special when presented with these pastries topped with sugared raspberries.

HERE'S HOW

1 Preheat oven to 375°F. In a mixing bowl combine the flour, baking powder, and salt. Using a pastry blender, cut in the shortening until the pieces are about the size of small peas.

2 Sprinkle 1 tablespoon of the milk over part of mixture; toss with fork. Push to side of bowl. Repeat until all is moistened. Divide into 6 portions. Shape into balls. Cover; set aside.

3 On a lightly floured surface, roll each ball to an 8-inch circle; trim to a 7½-inch circle. If you like, reserve trimmings for pastry leaves. Place an apple in the center of each circle.

4 Mix 1 cup sugar and the 1¼ teaspoons cinnamon. Sprinkle some of the mixture into the center of each apple. Top each with some of the 2 tablespoons butter.

5 Moisten the edges of pastry with some water. Bring dough up around each apple to form a bundle, pressing the edges together at the top to seal.

6 If desired, roll out dough trimmings; cut into leaf shapes. Brush tops of apple bundles with water; arrange leaves on top of each bundle, pressing into place. Place bundles in a lightly greased 3-quart rectangular baking dish.

7 In a saucepan combine 1½ cups sugar, the 1½ cups water, the ¼ teaspoon cinnamon, and nutmeg. Bring to boiling. Remove from heat; stir in 3 tablespoons butter. Pour over apples.

8 Bake in the preheated oven for 35 to 40 minutes or until done. If desired, trim with sugared cranberries. Serve warm with ice cream or cream. Makes 6.

Cranberry Strudel

WHAT YOU NEED

Strudel Dough (see page 287)

- 2 cups cranberries
- ½ cup dried apples, cut up
- ½ cup chopped pecans
- ¼ cup currants
- ¾ cup granulated sugar
- ¼ cup margarine or butter, melted
- 1 slightly beaten egg white
- 1 tablespoon water

    Powdered sugar

HERE'S HOW

1 Prepare Strudel Dough as directed. Meanwhile, in a medium saucepan combine cranberries and ¾ cup water. Bring to boiling. Reduce heat and simmer, uncovered, about 5 minutes or until cranberries pop; drain. In a bowl combine drained cranberries, dried apples, pecans, and currants. Add granulated sugar, then gently toss until mixed; set aside. Lightly grease a 15×10×1-inch baking pan; set aside.

2 To assemble strudel, stretch dough as directed on *page 287* and shown in Photo 1, *top right*. Brush stretched dough with melted margarine. Beginning 4 inches from a short side of dough, spoon filling in a 4-inch-wide band across dough as shown in Photo 2, *right*.

3 Preheat oven to 350°F. Using the cloth underneath the dough as a guide, gently lift the 4-inch edge of dough and lay it over the filling. Then slowly and evenly lift cloth and roll up the dough and filling into a tight roll as shown in Photo 3. If necessary, cut off excess dough from ends to within 1 inch of the filling. Fold ends under to seal.

4 Carefully transfer strudel roll to the prepared baking pan. Slightly curve the roll to form a crescent. Stir together egg white and water. Brush top of strudel with egg white mixture. Bake in the preheated oven for 35 to 40 minutes or until golden. Carefully remove strudel from pan and cool on a wire rack. Sift powdered sugar over strudel before serving. Serves 12 to 16.

Serve this dessert with small glasses of sherry.

1

2

3

277

Dried-Fruit Fruitcake

WHAT YOU NEED

1½ cups all-purpose flour
½ teaspoon baking powder
¼ teaspoon baking soda
½ cup margarine or butter
¾ cup packed brown sugar
2 eggs
1 teaspoon finely shredded orange peel
½ cup orange juice or apple juice
2 tablespoons light corn syrup
1 teaspoon vanilla
¾ cup snipped dried apricots
½ cup pitted whole dates, snipped
½ cup dried red cherries
½ cup chopped pecans or walnuts
   Brandy, or orange or apple juice

HERE'S HOW

1 Preheat oven to 300°F. Grease and lightly flour an 8-inch fluted tube mold. In a medium bowl combine flour, baking powder, and baking soda; set aside. In a large bowl beat margarine with a mixer on medium to high speed about 30 seconds or until softened. Add brown sugar; beat until combined. Add eggs, one at a time, beating on medium speed until combined. (Batter may appear curdled.) In a small bowl combine orange peel, the ½ cup orange juice, corn syrup, and vanilla. Alternately add flour mixture and orange juice mixture to margarine mixture, beating on low speed after each addition just until combined.

2 Combine apricots, dates, cherries, and pecans. Fold into batter. Spread in prepared pan. Bake in preheated oven about 1 hour or until cake tests done. (If necessary, cover loosely with foil for the last 15 to 30 minutes to prevent overbrowning.) Cool cake in tube mold on a wire rack for 10 minutes. Remove from pan; cool completely. Wrap cake in brandy-moistened 100-percent cotton cheesecloth. Place on a piece of foil; wrap well. Store on a plate in refrigerator for 2 to 8 weeks to mellow flavors. Remoisten cheesecloth with brandy or juice once a week or as needed. Serves 16.

This version features dried fruit instead of the traditional candied fruit.

ABOVE: *To remoisten fruitcake, partially unwrap it. With foil and cheesecloth around the base of the cake, spoon a small amount of brandy or fruit juice over cake. Rewrap cake, covering it with the moist cheesecloth and foil. Refrigerate for a week before remoistening again or rewrap until ready to serve.*

Buttercream Bûche de Noël

Prepared like a jelly roll, formed into a log shape, then cut into slices for serving, this hazelnut-orange dessert is a twist on the traditional chocolate Yule-log cake.

What You Need

1½ cups toasted hazelnuts
¼ cup all-purpose flour
6 egg yolks
⅔ cup packed brown sugar
2 teaspoons finely shredded orange peel
6 egg whites
¼ teaspoon cream of tartar
Powdered sugar
Caramel-Orange Buttercream
Sugared Cranberries; Chocolate Leaves

Here's How

1 Preheat oven to 350°F. Grease and lightly flour a 15×10×1-inch jelly-roll pan; set aside. In a food processor bowl combine the nuts and flour. Process until nuts are finely ground; set aside.

2 In a bowl beat egg yolks with mixer on high 6 minutes or until thick and lemon colored. Gradually add ⅓ cup of the brown sugar, beating on medium 5 minutes or until sugar is almost dissolved. Stir in peel; set aside. Wash beaters.

3 In a large bowl beat egg whites and cream of tartar on medium speed until soft peaks form. Gradually add the remaining brown sugar, beating until stiff peaks form. Fold yolk mixture into beaten egg whites. Sprinkle flour mixture into egg mixture and gently fold in by hand.

4 Spread batter evenly in pan. Bake in the preheated oven 15 to 20 minutes or until top springs back when lightly touched. Immediately loosen cake from pan. Invert onto a towel sprinkled with powdered sugar. Roll up warm cake and towel, jelly-roll style, starting from short side. Cool.

5 Gently unroll the cake. Spread 1¼ cups Caramel-Orange Buttercream on cake to within ½ inch of edges. Roll up cake without towel, starting from short side. Cut a 2-inch diagonal slice from one end. Place slice at side of log to form branch. Frost cake with remaining buttercream. Using a fork, score cake lengthwise to resemble tree bark. If desired, garnish with Sugared Cranberries and Chocolate

Leaves. Cover; store in the refrigerator up to 3 days.
Makes 10 servings.

6 **CARAMEL-ORANGE BUTTERCREAM:** In a medium saucepan
stir together ⅓ cup packed brown sugar and 2 tablespoons
cornstarch. Stir in 1¼ cups half-and-half or light cream.
Cook and stir over medium heat until thickened and
bubbly. Reduce heat; cook and stir 2 minutes more.
Gradually stir half of the mixture into 2 slightly beaten egg
yolks; return to remaining hot mixture. Bring to a gentle
boil. Cook and stir mixture for 2 minutes. Remove from
heat. Add 2 teaspoons finely shredded orange peel. Cover
surface with clear plastic wrap. Cool to room temperature.
Do not stir. In a mixing bowl beat ¾ cup softened butter
(no substitutes), ¾ cup sifted powdered sugar, and
1 tablespoon orange liqueur or orange juice with electric
mixer on medium speed until light and fluffy. Add cooled
cooked mixture, ¼ cup at a time, beating on low speed
after each addition until smooth.

7 **SUGARED CRANBERRIES:** For garnish only, dip cranberries
in lightly beaten egg white, then roll in granulated sugar.
Set aside to dry.

8 **CHOCOLATE LEAVES:** Use nontoxic leaves such as mint,
rose, lemon, or strawberry. For 12 small leaves, melt
2 ounces quick-tempered chocolate or melted baking bar
or candy coating. With a clean, small paintbrush, brush
one or two coats of melted chocolate onto underside of
each leaf. Wipe away any chocolate from top side of leaf.
Place leaves, chocolate side up, on a curved surface or
waxed-paper-lined baking sheet until dry. Before using,
peel leaf away from chocolate.

Poached Pears

For a stunning dessert that tastes heavenly, it is hard to outdo an exquisite poached pear. Whole pears are poached in a caramel-orange sauce, then topped with Crème Anglaise, a sumptuous vanilla-flavored custard.

WHAT YOU NEED

⅓ cup brown sugar
¼ cup orange juice
½ teaspoon ground nutmeg
1 tablespoon amaretto or ½ teaspoon almond extract
6 ripe medium pears
1 cup granulated sugar
2 cups warm Crème Anglaise
⅓ cup sliced almonds, toasted
Fresh mint leaves

HERE'S HOW

1 In a large skillet stir together brown sugar, orange juice, and nutmeg. Cook and stir over low heat until sugar is melted. Bring to boiling; gently boil 3 to 4 minutes or until reduced to half. Stir in amaretto. Set aside.

2 Peel pears, leaving stems on. Core pears from bottoms. In a medium saucepan bring 3 cups water and granulated sugar to boiling. Carefully add pears, stem ends up. Reduce heat. Cover and simmer 20 minutes or until pears are tender. Remove saucepan from heat and let pears cool in liquid.

3 Transfer pears to individual serving dishes. Pour warm Crème Anglaise around pears. Drizzle caramel-orange mixture over pears. Sprinkle with almonds and garnish with fresh mint leaves. Makes 6 servings.

4 CRÈME ANGLAISE: In a heavy saucepan bring 1⅓ cups whipping cream and 1 vanilla bean, split lengthwise, just to boiling, stirring frequently. Remove from heat. In a mixing bowl combine small amount of hot cream mixture, 2 egg yolks, and ⅔ cup sugar. Beat with an electric mixer on high speed 2 to 3 minutes or until thick and lemon-colored. Gradually stir about half of remaining cream mixture into egg yolk mixture. Return egg yolk mixture to saucepan. Cook and stir over medium heat just to boiling. Remove from heat. Discard vanilla bean. If desired, stir in 1 tablespoon amaretto or orange liqueur. Makes 2 cups.

Christmas Tree Care

BALSAM FIR

DOUGLAS FIR

SCOTCH PINE

TIPS FOR CHOOSING YOUR TREE AND EXTENDING ITS LIFE

Nothing says Christmas like an evergreen tree decorated with ornaments, lights, and tinsel. To make the best selection, look for a fragrant tree with resilient, green needles and a trunk that's sticky with sap. Needles should stay on even when you shake the tree, and branches should not break easily, unless the tree is frozen.

Before you buy a tree, give it this test:

- Examine the needles. Hold a branch in your hand and pull it toward you, allowing it to slip through your fingers. If several needles fall into your hand, don't buy the tree.
- Smell the tree. If it's fresh, the moisture content will keep it fragrant.
- Check the color. A healthy, fresh tree will have a good green color.
- Peek at the trunk. It should be sticky with sap.

Whether you visit a choose-and-cut tree farm or your favorite stand in town, hunting for the perfect Christmas tree can be a fun holiday tradition for the whole family. If you're not sure what type to choose, here are some characteristics to consider:

- Balsam and Douglas firs are aromatic and have a pyramid shape.
- Scotch pines are busy, dense trees with short needles that cling to the branches.
- Red cedars rarely drop a needle.
- Eastern white pines have pretty, slender blue needles, but the branches can be flimsy.

Once the tree is home, place it in your garage or basement to let it acclimate to the warmth of your home. Cut a ¼-inch diagonal slice from the tree base to break the seal of sap and to let moisture in.

If you aren't planning to decorate the tree immediately, put it in a large bucket of water. When you're ready to trim the tree, cut another thick disk from the bottom of the trunk, making it flat for stability. Set the tree in a stand that will hold at least a gallon of water, and water the tree regularly. A 6-foot tree can drink up to one gallon of water the first 24 hours and 2 quarts of water a day thereafter. If you interrupt watering even one day, the tree will dry out rapidly and may not rebound after the water supply is replenished.

Place the tree away from heat sources such as fireplaces, television sets, and radiators. Mist the tree occasionally to keep the branches fresh.

RED CEDAR

RECYCLING TIPS

Don't burn a spent tree in an indoor fireplace—the foliage is dangerously flammable. Instead, put the tree to work around your home.

- Extend the life of branches that are still green. Cut these away from the tree and place them in a bucket of water to regain moisture; assemble into wreaths.
- Cut off branches and chop up trunk to make garden mulch. Use around plants that prefer acidic soil such as hydrangeas and blueberries.
- Put the tree in the garden or backyard and turn it into a bird feeder and shelter by adding suet, orange slices, and other treats.
- Lay your tree and others in gullies to control erosion by holding organic debris. If you live on a lake, spread your tree and others along the beachfront to encourage development of sand dunes.

WHITE PINE

Index